THE FISHERMAN'S
APPRENTICE

To Nigel Legge – my mentor and friend.
To John, Tonks, Worm, Louis, Danny, Mitch, Dom, Jonathan,
Philip, Luke and George.
To Tony and Peter – still on their voyage.

Finally to my daughter Isla Grace, in the sincere hope that she grows up
to see fishing boats on the beach at Cadgwith.

THE FISHERMAN'S
APPRENTICE
Monty Halls

This book is published to accompany the television series entitled *The Fisherman's Apprentice*, first broadcast on BBC TWO in 2012. The series was produced for BBC television by Indus Films Ltd.

10 9 8 7 6 5 4 3 2 1

Published by AA Publishing, a trading name of AA Media Limited, whose registered office is Fanum House, Basing View, Basingstoke RG21 4EA. Registered number 06112600.

Cover photography and picture editor – James Tims
Layout – Nick Johnston
Picture researcher – Alice Earle
Digital imaging and repro – Jacqueline Street
Editorial support – Clare Ashton and Karen Rigden
Copy editor – Caroline Taggart
Indexer – Hilary Bird
Concept design – Smith & Gilmour
Map illustrations © Scott Jessop Illustration
Contains Ordnance Survey data © Crown copyright and database right 2012

We support the Forest Stewardship Council (FSC®), the leading international forest certification organisation. Our books carrying the FSC label are printed on FSC certified paper. FSC is the only forest certification scheme endorsed by the leading environmental organisations, including Greenpeace.

A CIP catalogue record for this book is available from the British Library.

ISBN 978-0-7495-7272-3

Printed and bound in Great Britain by Butler Tanner & Dennis, Frome, Somerset.

Find out more about AA Publishing and the wide range of services the AA provides by visiting our website at theAA.com/shop

A04774

CONTENTS

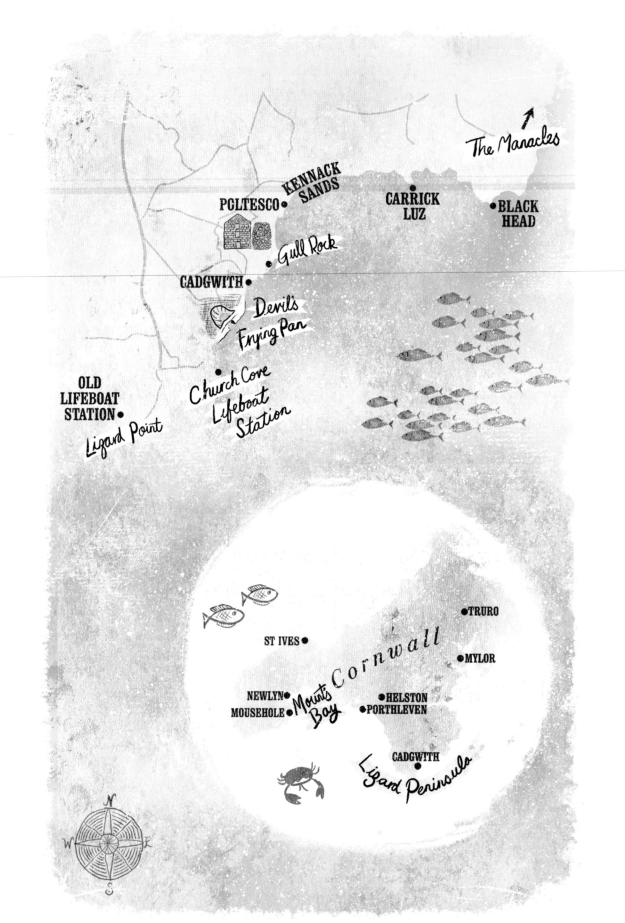

INTRODUCTION

Our fishing fleet places our island nation in something of a dilemma. Although it is rather distant to most of us, we nonetheless have a romantic notion of what it does and why it's important. Yet we still tend to form our opinions from the media and certain well-established clichés.

So on the one hand, we feel a certain sense of pride and benevolent partnership with the bustling, brightly coloured vessels that putter along our coastline. After all, we remain an island race, intimately connected to the sea even in this technological age. On the other hand, we lump our fishermen into one massive group of oilskin-clad men who sing in close harmony and work fiendish hours. We regard the small boat handlining for bass a mile off Weymouth in much the same light as the monster beam trawler powering out of Hull.

Whether inshore or offshore, using static pots or trawled gear, in recent years the fishing fleets *en masse* have been seen in a negative light, with campaigns that portray them mercilessly ploughing the seabed, circling tuna schools and attendant pods of dolphins, hacking the fins off sharks, obliterating huge shoals of vulnerable species and generally ravaging ecosystems. The impression is of a ruthless industry that is pillaging the ocean in a last-ditch attempt to make the most of a vanishing resource at a time of rising legislation and increased running costs.

These notions are similar to the schizophrenic attitude we seem to apply to our farming community. In one moment they are noble, down-trodden, honest yeomen tilling the earth to feed the nation. In the next they are villainous, badger-murdering, grant-grabbing capitalists, bent on ravaging the natural environment, tampering with genetics and fleecing the EU.

As a marine conservationist, I was more than aware of the arguments raised against our fishermen, and yet in coming to the tiny Cornish fishing village of Cadgwith I was about to learn their story from the inside out.

I quickly discovered that eight out of ten of the fishing vessels that work our inshore waters are less than 10 metres long, a far cry from mighty beam trawlers and factory ships. And the fishermen operate within the rules laid down by legislation, which often demands that they shovel much of their catch back overboard. The vast majority of fishermen are the latest in an ancestral line and want nothing more than to hand their boats on to their sons so they too can fish in vibrant, healthy seas. They have become the villains in the drama, and yet generally speaking there is no one keener on keeping the fishing grounds around Britain healthy and productive than the fishermen themselves. Why would they want it any other way? It is, after all, their livelihood.

But the sad news is that today we are looking at the demise of the fishing industry as we know it. At the heart of the industry is an impossible matrix of contradictory data from scientific bodies, the fishermen themselves and various legislative groups. Much of this data is based on attempts to monitor populations of fish species that we still don't entirely understand, to gather information from the vast echoing spaces of the open ocean and to deal with organisations that speak entirely different languages and have different political agendas. This

'We remain an island race, intimately connected to the sea even in this technological age' information is then passed onto big businesses and lobbying groups to make changes that they don't want to make in timescales that aren't reasonable. That's the complex reality.

The simple reality, of course, is that there are just not enough fish left, and we have to do something about it or we're in real trouble.

The UN reports that 32 per cent of global fish stocks are seriously over-exploited, and that 90 per cent of large species such as tuna and marlin have been fished to the point of extinction over the last hundred years. We catch about 80 million tonnes of fish a year and, although this seems to have plateaued since the mid 1990s, the problem is that there are a lot more of us eating a lot more of them. In the 1960s our global seafood consumption was 10 kilograms per person each year. Today it is 17 kilograms.

In European waters the picture is even less rosy. We're at the end of a fishing spree that has lasted thousands of years, reaping a glittering harvest from the cold, rich waters of the eastern Atlantic. The Marine Conservation Society estimates that 72 per cent of European fish stocks are now being fished at levels that are simply not sustainable. The response has been a series of impenetrable and nonsensical laws passed down in a 'top-down, one-size-fits-all' style of management that has seen – just by way of an example – £1 billion worth of North Sea cod discarded back into the sea by British fishing boats alone since 1963, part of the £2.7 billion total that has been thrown back if you take vessels from other nations into the equation.

I had been campaigning for a number of years to get Marine Nature Reserves set up around the UK and, although I had never regarded the fishing fleet as the enemy (an attitude adopted by certain terminally dim members of the conservation lobby), there was no denying that our agendas were different. I was all in favour of No-Take Zones, and restrictions on fishing in certain areas and for certain species. In stark contrast, the fishing lobby obviously felt they could manage their own industry more capably than a group of people who had never been on a fishing boat in their lives, knew nothing about the unique pressures and perils of their way of life and were out of touch with the realities of the local stocks that fishing communities monitored every working day as part of their next shift on the job.

So joining the fishing fleet was a bit of a leap in the dark for me. I thought I knew about the impact of fishing on the marine environment, but the information I had garnered had all come from the conservation lobby. It was a bit like joining the Conservatives having been briefed on their policies by Labour. Spending the coming months in Cadgwith was to transform the way I looked at the British fishing industry, our oceans and indeed myself. And yet the conservation dilemmas remained – with one, massive, overarching question throughout. Could our fishermen move into the future working in a sustainable, environmentally friendly industry and yet continue to supply the immense demands of the market?

The one thing I could never have anticipated was just how immersed I would become in the plight of these fishermen. But it was on a beautiful spring day in Cornwall that the true story of our small-scale fishing industry began to unfold for me.

'Eight out of ten of the fishing vessels that work our inshore waters are less than 10 metres long'

THE DEFIANT OUTPOST

CHAPTER 1

The road had become almost impossibly tight, snaking and twisting in a series of switchbacks and hairpins as I dropped towards the ragged edge of England.

I was driving to the very tip of our island, a finger of rock made crooked by wind and wave, pointing into the heart of the Atlantic. The landscape around me was a riot of colour, with every passing meadow in full bloom following the warmest spring in a hundred years. My wing mirrors brushed through the hedgerows as the road narrowed into a green valley, hemmed in by steep banks of bramble flowers and willow-herb. These ravines had been carved by the passage of foot, wagon and car over many generations, and the vertical walls now trapped the heady scent of wild basil, garlic and thyme that crowded in on either side.

This had been a long journey for me in every sense and, as the Land Rover gears crunched and my foot pumped on the brakes, I reflected on the many miles and several years that had led me to this place. The steering wheel spun and bucked in my hands as I negotiated yet another tight turn – then suddenly before me I saw Cadgwith Cove for the very first time.

I pulled into a lay-by and switched off the engine, leaving it to cool gently with a series of metallic ticks as I stepped out to peer at the scene below. The air was rich with the myriad scents of a temperate May, humming with insects moving in lazy spirals along the edge of the road, while the surf on the beach below rustled and whispered on the shingle of the cove.

Even from the most cursory glance, I could see how the village of Cadgwith had been moulded by the landscape on which it was built. It sits on the Lizard Peninsula, an impossibly dramatic series of cliffs, crags and fissures that speak of tectonic forces and elemental storms. It's an environment shaped by violence and brokers no compromise for those who choose to make it their home. Cadgwith crowds in upon itself, rising in tiers from the beach at all angles, clinging to the sides of the valley that leads inland from the cove itself.

On this spring day it created a striking picture, with thatched cottages shining white in the sun, and brightly painted boats leaning drunkenly on the beach as though weary after their day's work on the blue water. Rows of gulls roosted on top of a pub, bills buried deep in the down of their puffed-out chests, eyes half shut as the wind ruffled their feathers.

That the colourful fishing fleet sits at the heart of Cadgwith is entirely appropriate: it represents the essence of the community, the point from which all other activities spring. The very name of the village speaks of its ancient bond to the sea. 'Cadgwith' is a coarse evolution of the ancient Cornish word *Porthcaswith*, first recorded in 1360 and translated as 'the landing place of the thicket'. The valley leading inland from the village – the thicket of so many centuries before – remains absurdly green and lush, the result of warm winds and cold sea mists. And yet the brook at its heart meanders towards the shore, drawn irresistibly to the sea – as with all things on the Lizard – to dissipate on the loose stones of the beach.

It was a scene straight from my childhood, an evocative assault on my senses that sparked distant memories of

holidays when the sun shone and the sea held the promise of adventure and impossibly exotic travel beyond its wide horizon. Those initial forays into the sea, those first faltering explorations of rock pools and shallows, had set in motion a chain of events that ultimately led to my becoming a diver and marine biologist. An enthusiastic child had run shrieking with excitement towards the surf all those years before, but it was an embryonic scientist who had come back, the path of his life firmly set, even though he remained blissfully unaware of it at the time.

'Cadgwith is one of the last truly artisanal fishing villages in Britain'

But as I looked down upon Cadgwith I didn't feel the usual sense of excitement – there was none of the normal desperate urge to push towards the sea. Instead I felt raw nerves, a sick anticipation at the challenge ahead. I knew this was not just another quaint village tucked into a Cornish cove. I was looking at an outpost, a bastion, a fortress sitting on a border between two different worlds and two different cultures.

Cadgwith is one of the last truly artisanal fishing villages in Britain, the eight fishing boats on the beach representing another way of life, distant from the bedlam and industry of the modern world. The men who skipper and crew these boats were the latest in a line of fishermen working from that same beach – a line that stretched back a thousand years. They were a breed of their own, a proud tribe that still fished in a sustainable, uniquely co-operative manner. Their language and culture had developed

in the enclosed environment of the cove, echoing off the rock walls for generation after generation. Over the coming months, I was planning to become one of their number, attempting to make the unlikely transformation from a work-shy, soft-palmed ex-public school boy into a Cornish fisherman working the Atlantic off the tip of a mighty headland.

Time was rolling on, with the soft sunlight of a spring morning giving way to the hard glare of midday. Climbing back into the Land Rover, I started the engine one last time, pulled out of the lay-by and dropped the final few hundred yards into the heart of the village.

* * *

To understand Cadgwith and the men who make their living from the sea here, you must first understand the Lizard. By coincidence, one of the rocks historically mined here is serpentine, so named because its surface resembles the scales of a snake. Such a reptilian theme seems entirely appropriate for the landscape from which it is drawn, with great Jurassic cliffs plunging into wild seas.

The Lizard Peninsula is an undeniably beautiful place – a tumbling collection of towering buttresses, dark rocks and sinuous paths. But all the while something deadly lies beneath. It is a landscape twisted and contorted by unimaginable power, its seams welded together by continental drift and its rheumatic features the result of geological uplift and wild, elemental storms.

The Lizard is nothing more than a ragged salient thrust into the no-man's land of the Atlantic. To fish off this coast is to pitch and toss close to crackling rock walls, with the sea's surface seething and booming into angled gullies and narrow fissures. It is an

entirely different place from almost anywhere else in England and, as with everything grand and scenic, there is something implacable about it. To stand on one of the high cliffs and watch the sea beneath is to be simultaneously thrilled and appalled, fascinated not only by the wonder of the setting, but also by its power and its latent ability to destroy.

During my research I'd learned that the Lizard Peninsula is the best-preserved example of an exposed ophiolite in the United Kingdom. This sounded tremendously exciting but I had no idea what an ophiolite was. Reading my guidebook on arrival, I discovered it meant 'a suite of geological formations which represent a slice of the ocean's crust thrust into the continental mantle'. I'm sure this makes perfect sense if you're a geologist, but for a chap expecting mystical menhirs of sparkling quartz surrounded by chanting druids, it was something of a let-down.

It turns out that the grandeur of the Lizard, and the sensation that you have arrived somewhere faintly otherworldly, owes much to this feature. An ophiolite brings to the surface rocks that normally seethe in the heat of the mantle many kilometres underground. When they do see the light of day, many of them – serpentine included – are poor in nutrients and difficult to farm, and so great swathes of the Lizard remain uncultivated, offering a glimpse of a landscape unchanged by the ordering hand of man.

The geological quirk that is an ophiolite was not overlooked by the ancient inhabitants of the Lizard. Clay mined from between the inlets of Coverack and Kennack was of a particularly fine quality and has been found in pots throughout the UK and as far away as Brittany. These were

produced in Neolithic times, mind you, so it would appear that even then the locals were selling bits and bobs to tourists. I could almost imagine the conversation.

'Go on, it's from an exposed ophiolite, you know.'

'All right then, chuck in the stone club and you've got a deal. Blimey, it looks a bit like a snake. I'll take two.'

Perhaps it's no surprise that historically the people who have made their home on the Lizard have been something of a fierce and proud bunch. The Cornish rebellion started here in 1497 when a local blacksmith, Michael Joseph, became outraged that Henry VII was raising taxes to fund the war against the Scots.

Showing commendable ambition but a lamentable grasp of tactics, Michael decided to march on London with his mate Thomas Flamack and a modest band of followers. They were duly routed and the two leaders hanged, drawn and quartered. I imagine at least 25 per cent of Michael would have looked faintly preoccupied as it was strung up, making a belated mental note not to march on capital cities and incumbent monarchs armed with nothing more than a sense of moral outrage and a funny-shaped hammer.

The poor quality of the soil also means that much of the peninsula has simply been left to grow wild. Bog and heath, meadow and hedgerow have all run riot, with a patchwork of colours competing for the attention of insects that weave in narcotic spirals from flower to flower. The pink of rosebay willowherb contrasts with the purple of musk thistle and the white of switchwort, while yellow primrose and Hottentot figs shimmer and twitch in the gentle sea breeze. At the very edge of the cliffs the plants jostle for space, springing from every nook and cranny, with increasingly fibrous stems and stiff petals as the edge beckons. The epitome of this is thrift, a stumpy pink flower that grows in aggressive clumps on the cliff walls, vibrating vigorously and looking rather annoyed at the impact of the surf only yards away.

As the very first landfall after the wide open spaces of the Atlantic, and bathed in the warm waters of the Gulf Stream, the peninsula is home to some unique wildlife. To sit on the cliffs is to rest in the midst of 1,662 hectares of National Nature Reserve, a front-row seat from which to look out upon whales, dolphins, basking sharks and sunfish. Glance down at your generously supported rump and you may well be looking at Cornish heather, riotously abundant here, but found nowhere else in Britain. Slit your eyes to peer through the fronds and you may see the narrow-headed ant, once again unique to the Lizard. Glance upwards and there is every chance you will see a chough effortlessly surfing the barrelling upwellings of the sea winds ricocheting off the cliffs. With its red legs and orange beak it is completely distinctive – although just to remind you it will shout its own name over and over like some temperamental toddler.

As if all this wasn't enough, the Lizard also has plenty of drama going on in the water that surrounds it. Look out towards a deep-blue horizon and you are viewing the scene of many an epic ocean tragedy.

The Lizard juts out in a thoroughly inconvenient manner if you happen to be a skipper making for the deep-water harbour of Falmouth. It represents a trap, carefully constructed by Mother Nature, where tides, waves, winds and hidden reefs combine to ensnare hapless vessels. The wrecks scattered and broken on the reefs represent a history of seafaring, from elegant schooners to modern trawlers.

The rocks and outcrops in this region all bear names that speak of dark deeds on stormy nights – the Manacles, Craggan Rocks, Black Head, the Bears, the Gear and, perhaps most ominously of all, one ragged peak known simply as the Stone. These are names that would haunt helmsmen as the cliffs of Cornwall hove into view, and all have claimed their share of the unwary or the unlucky.

The Lizard Lighthouse stands sentinel on the very southern tip of the peninsula, its light sweeping above the maelstrom directly beneath as tide meets wind, with shallow reefs causing the waters to seethe and thrash in a series of standing waves and mini whirlpools directly off the point. Lifeboats have conducted some of the most remarkable and heroic rescues in the history of the RNLI from these waters, almost always returning home against all the odds. Almost. But not always.

Cadgwith sits tucked into the south-eastern edge of the peninsula. The entrance to Cadgwith Cove is cupped by towering cliffs on either side that lower abruptly into a shingle beach split by a rocky outcrop called the Todden. This is big enough for a cluster of small cottages to be built at its base, and for tourists to sit on a weathered wooden bench at its tip – a perfect rocky jetty thrusting into the sea, splitting the swells that snarl and tumble along it. This perch allows day trippers in

Bog and heath, meadow and hedgerow have all run riot, with a patchwork of colours competing for the attention of insects floppy hats to lick ice creams while looking down on the fishing fleet surfing expertly ashore within yards of their feet.

The village's relatively sheltered location permits the fleet to launch on any day when the wind is westerly, slipping past the Todden into waters that lie in the lee of the high ground behind them. It is this geological feature that has sometimes allowed the Cadgwith fleet to keep fishing when others cannot, patiently combing the calm waters close to home, moving in the shadow of the cliffs that offer them protection.

But when the winds increase or shift, then the boats remain marooned on the beach, with a vicious chopping surge snapping at their heels as the waves are channelled and focused by the narrow walls of the cove. By the time the surge hits the beach it is full of venom and purpose, hissing at the shingle and coveting the fleet. On these days the fishermen tinker with their pots and their nets, gathering to talk quietly as their money silently haemorrhages away. A day on the beach is a day with no pay. String too many of those together and bankruptcy beckons – and so they stare, they pace, they mutter and always they look to the skies.

* * *

My guide and mentor for my transition into a Cadgwith fisherman was to be Nigel Legge. Nigel had been fishing the cove all his life, just as his father had before him, and indeed his before him. Nigel could trace his ancestry back to the very origins of Cadgwith, and at an extremely well preserved 61 years of age had witnessed many changes in the fleet even in his own lifetime. He had kindly agreed to take me on as his apprentice, offering me a chance to work on his boat before taking her over

for a short trial period. We all use the term 'local legend' rather idly, but Nigel was the real deal, a cross between Gandalf and Obi-Wan Kenobi, with a slight whiff of lobster and sea salt thrown in. I was very excited about meeting him for the first time.

That first meeting would need to wait just a little longer, as I had to settle into the accommodation that would serve as my home for the period of my apprenticeship. This was an old net store above a converted pilchard cellar. I had envisaged a scene of Dickensian gloom but my new quarters were actually very nice indeed.

Reflecting the modern reality of a great many coastal communities in latter-day Cornwall, the Old Cellars had been converted into a beautiful little holiday home. The loft where the nets had once been stored was now a long room redolent of dark wood. At one end, in front of two gigantic sofas, stood a wood-burning stove. Atmospherically soft levels of natural light were created by four beautiful casement windows, making the wood of the floor gently shine. It looked like a haven, a bolt hole, and indeed in the months to come there would be many occasions when the door would crash open as I stumbled in, a ruin of a man.

The original cellars had been created at the height of the pilchard boom, an extraordinary period in the history of fishing in Cornwall when catches were measured in their millions, a glittering harvest that utterly transformed the community and culture. My new home was part of a complex of buildings created in the late 18th century to process the catch and store the fishing gear.

The last truly great pilchard hauls took place in the early 1900s, and then the immense shoals on which the industry

depended simply vanished. The old fishermen said the wind had changed, or the water temperature and currents had altered, but perhaps the truth is more sinister. In nearby St Ives fishermen took 30 million pilchards in a single hour – leaving the stocks heavily depleted. Can any species stand such immense fishing pressure? The truth is that no one really knows where the pilchards went, but their disappearance sounded a warning that still echoes across history, showing the folly of eradicating vast aggregations of any single animal.

The communities that had been created to exploit the pilchards flexed and evolved; today the mechanisms of fishing have been altered to serve the latest great migration to Cornish shores – tourists. Below my apartment was a delightful little cafe and restaurant, so as I strode about after a day's fishing my festering bare feet would be only inches above the sunburned heads of diners polishing off crab salads and cream teas. Occasionally my afternoon work would be interrupted by the smell of coffee wafting through the floorboards. This would be accompanied by the unmistakable sound of a coffee machine and barista banging out a double-strength latte, a sound which punctuated my afternoons more and more as the holiday season got into full swing.

If the cafe was close by, the pub was virtually part of my bedroom. From the base of my bed to the beer garden was about four feet, with only a window and the narrowest of alleys separating the two spaces. I would often wonder what the drinkers made of a large semi-clad man stumbling about with one sock on looking for his pants as they supped their pint only yards away. This sleeping arrangement also gave me the unmissable opportunity

'This was the man who would shape my next year, who would have to mould me into something approaching a semblance of himself'

to listen to drunk people's discussions night after night. You know when you've had a few and think you're being particularly funny, pithy and erudite? Well, after months and months of research, allow me to be the first to tell you that you're probably not.

* * *

Having dropped my bags off in the loft, I made my way down to the beach. Nigel was tinkering with his boat close to the surf line, so I weaved between the remainder of the fleet towards him. There were no other fishermen around, and he glanced up as my feet crunched over the shingle. On seeing me approach he vaulted over the side of the boat and stood four square on the beach, one hand extended. This was the man who would shape my next year, who would have to mould me into something approaching a semblance of himself, and who would keep me safe from the venomous fangs of the Lizard. I awaited his first utterance with bated breath, the disciple meeting the master.

'Well I'll be, you're a big bugger. I can get you to lift a few heavy things if nothing else.' He smiled broadly and shook me firmly by the hand. Then he turned to look at the fleet pulled up on the shingle, gesturing expansively to the row of garishly coloured sterns and the cottages beyond, before turning back to me and smiling once again. 'Welcome to Cadgwith, young man.'

Nigel Legge – Nige – looked every inch the archetypal Cornish fisherman. He wore a tattered blue sweater emblazoned with red letters that proudly declared 'RNLI', over the top of which was a set of soiled and creased oilskin dungarees. It dawned on me that you had to earn both of those items of clothing – the sweater through dedication and selflessness, and the battered dungarees through hard work. Nige had a shock of white hair that stood out in all manner of interesting angles, contrasting with the deep tan of his face, creased by a lifetime of squinting at the sea ahead and crisscrossed with distinct laughter lines. A piratical gold earring dangled from one ear, glinting in the morning sun. He gave the impression of great solidity and strength, as though decades of balancing on canting decks had created a certain – dare I say it – balletic economy of movement.

The great clarion call for the modern fitness trainer is for core strength, and in this there can be no finer training ground than a boat at sea, with a lobster pot in one hand and various laws of physics pulling you in several exhilarating directions at once. Fishermen are not just strong, they have to constantly balance and compensate, to adjust and correct. If you're going to have a fight with a fisherman – always, always a bad idea – make sure it doesn't happen on roller skates, a bouncy castle or a trampoline.

Nige looked out towards the sea and then back to me.

'Right, Mont,' – the little phrase that, unbeknown to me, would prelude some of the more interesting moments of my life over the coming months – 'I reckon we should go out to sea. You up for it?'

In anticipation of precisely this event I had put on several layers of extra clothes, topped by a windproof jacket. I may have overdone it slightly and realised in retrospect that I was actually dressed for a single-handed attempt to encircle Antarctica. With that in mind I figured that puttering out of Cadgwith onto a glassy Cornish sea for an hour with the most experienced fisherman on the Lizard would be a risk worth taking. I nodded wordlessly, threw my bag into the boat and looked back expectantly towards Nige.

'There can be no finer training ground than a boat at sea, with a lobster pot in one hand and various laws of physics pulling you in several exhilarating directions at once'

'This,' he said, slapping the colourful transom behind him, 'is *Razorbill*. She's one of the smallest boats working off the coast of Cornwall, but she's kept me safe for 20 years or so and does a damn fine job.' He smiled proprietarily and looked at me for some sort of response.

Razorbill was a robust 18-footer painted a fetching snow white, with a light-blue edge around her open deck. A shining cylindrical winch stood proud of her bow, while at her stern a russet-coloured sail was wrapped around a small mizzen mast. She looked very business-like, but nonetheless rather friendly in the style of an aging maiden aunt. She had no cabin or wheelhouse at all, although I suspect given the right set of circumstances I could probably have squeezed into the forward compartment, which was about the size of a tiny drawer.

Her keel was covered by a long band of steel, alongside which ran two further supports that also had a metal strip at their base. The boats of Cadgwith spend their days being hauled up over the stones of the beach and need runners both to move smoothly and to avoid having their hulls worn away over time. At her stern was a simple tiller mechanism, beneath which shone a brass propeller.

'She's lovely, Nige,' I said, and meant it. His smile broadened.

'Let's get her in then, shall we? I've got a few pots to haul and I can show you a bit of the coast. Treat this first outing as a cruise – after this you're on the clock.' He winked, leapt athletically aboard a nearby tractor, gunned the engine and, with considerable scrunching of shingle and crunching of gears, pushed *Razorbill* by her bow into the shallows.

> 'The spectre of those lost to the sea is a constant companion, their memory immortalised in the names of local reefs or sandbars, or in weathered plaques cemented into harbour walls'

He stopped the tractor engine, the abrupt silence amplified by walls around us, climbed out of the cab and vaulted over *Razorbill*'s bow to start her up. It was beginning to occur to me that Nige's life consisted of a great deal of acrobatic leaping about, and his effortless boarding of the boat contrasted sharply with my own slithering, grunting entrance, landing on the deck with flapping oilskins followed by a long, wide-eyed skid towards the stern as one of my new wellie-boot heels connected with something slimy and unpleasant underfoot.

Razorbill reversed sharply away from the beach, then turned a neat 180 degrees as Nigel leaned on the tiller. She pointed her bright bow at the distant horizon and we were away.

As we edged out from the protection of the rock walls that surrounded the cove, I felt some of my fears drop away. There is something primal about setting out to sea, even if only for short trip such as this – the first of many for me in *Razorbill*. Cornwall is a beautiful place, and the Lizard one of its most enchanting areas, but you only really appreciate just how lovely it all is when you are in a small boat beneath the towering buttresses of great cliffs. As we turned to run close to shore, Nige pointed out various interesting nooks and crannies on the rock walls, all of them lined and fissured with old age. They stood glowering and timeless as the seas heaved against their base, our tiny boat lost in their shadows.

Having turned a sharp right out of the cove, we were soon faced with a huge and impressive rock arch under which the water echoed and thumped.

'Aha,' said Nige, 'now this is the Devil's Frying Pan. Go in here when it's stormy and you'll have a brief but extremely exciting fishing trip.' He gave a bark of laughter, his voice booming around the rock walls. I glanced into the water and saw the walls of the arch slipping away beneath the boat, glowing an eerie bottle green as the light danced and pulsed on the surface of the sea above.

As we turned away from the entrance to the main chamber, with *Razorbill* having performed a tidy pirouette within the confines of the tight walls, Nige pointed out a dark rock that protruded through the surface of the sea like a jagged tooth.

'See that? We call that the Johnny Carter Rock.'

I nearly said something flippant, a throwaway line about dodgy navigation and some hapless fisherman having to buy a round in the Cadgwith Cove Inn. But something stopped me, some dark shadow that passed behind Nige's eyes as he spoke. He paused for a beat before continuing.

'Yeah, some poor soul called Johnny Carter had his boat wrecked in a storm and managed to swim to that rock. He was rescued, but died when they got him to the beach.' He paused again before appearing to shake himself out of his reverie. 'Long time ago, mind. Let's push on up the coast, shall we?'

As with any fishing community, the spectre of those lost to the sea is a constant companion, their memory immortalised in the names of local reefs or sandbars, or in weathered plaques cemented into harbour walls. There wasn't a fisherman in Cadgwith who hadn't lost a friend at sea, and as my time in the village progressed I would learn that the great rewards of this life, of the idyll we imagine is the existence of a Cornish fisherman, are hard earned indeed.

We puttered back across the face of the cove again, this time heading for a distant headland that loomed far off in the shimmering heat. It was about three miles away, hunched and uniform with its dark shoulders in shadow leading to an impressively craggy headland broken into a series of reefs and protruding rocks.

'That's Black Head. It's about the limit of where you'll put your pots. Go any further and you'll not only be placing your fishing gear in an area I don't know that well...' (Sounds interesting, I thought.) 'you'll also

probably get punched on the nose by some of the lads from the next village along.' (Best stick to Black Head, I thought.)

As we motored away from the cove, I watched it vanish behind the steep wall of the cliffs. We passed a great pinnacle of rock that rose from the surface of the sea, its surface snow white with centuries of guano. Atop the rock stood a huge flock of gulls, bickering and basking in the late-afternoon light.

'We call that Gull Rock. Can't think why,' said Nige. 'By the way, did you see the way I turned her there as we set out from the beach? We always turn that way in the cove. Make sure your stern is towards the Todden and you'll be going the right way.'

This was actually a prelude to a number of customs and superstitions that peppered our short trip, ones that Nige reeled off as we pootled along towards the distant outline of Black Head.

'Right, Mont,' he said, once *Razorbill* had settled to her work and was moving sharply ahead of a bustling wake, 'I can't help noticing that you're wearing lots of green. Bad luck at sea that is, so next time we're out can you make sure anything green is left back on land.'

'But Nige,' I pointed out hesitantly, 'you're wearing green wellies.'

'They're not green,' he said firmly. 'They're olive.'

'But I'm sure I saw a green boat on the beach. Surely that's bad luck?'

'That's Louis' boat, and it's not green, it's mint. Right, the next thing is you must never, ever mention underground racehorses.'

I looked baffled.

'You know, those long-eared furry things.' Nige held up his hands and did a passable impression of what was unmistakably a rabbit.

'What, you mean rabbits?' I asked innocently.

'Oh my God,' said Nige, with genuine feeling, 'never say that word on *Razorbill* again. It's terribly bad luck. Really, Monts.' He looked at me aghast before continuing.

'Now, the next thing is pasties. Never take a pasty onto a boat while you're in Cornwall. If you absolutely have to board a boat with one, make sure you stab it first.'

Obviously, I thought, makes sense. I hesitated once again before revealing to Nige that I had innocently placed a pasty in my bag before jumping aboard.

'Oh my God, we're on a doomed boat!' he said with a half smile. 'Right, that's not a pasty, Mont, that's plainly a meat and potato pie. Let's just say no more after today, okay? And should you see a man of the cloth, a priest, on the morning you're due to go out to sea, don't go. Oh, and naturally women out at sea are bad luck for any boat, but I suspect you know that already.'

Some of these traditions and super-stitions surrounding the fishing fleet are based on religion, some on practicality, some on folklore and some have origins that are lost in the mists of time. Nige patiently explained most of them to me, although many must have seemed completely obvious to him. The turning in the cove follows the track of the sun across the sky, as an ancient myth decreed that witches would always fly against the direction of the sun.

They would also turn themselves into hares when on land, hence the aversion to rabbits. Not going to sea if you pass a priest on the way to the boat is fairly intuitive – it is, after all, the priest who oversees your funeral, and you don't want to tempt fate. Women not going to sea is also quite an obvious one, as women would traditionally look after the family and perform jobs ashore. Lose a boat, a tragically all-too-common occurrence before the days of the long-distance forecast, and if the husband and wife are both on board suddenly you have children in the village with no parents.

The pasty rule is slightly more tricky.

'Well, it'd just be a crumbly mess if it was raining or stormy, wouldn't it?' Nige suggested. 'Maybe it's because it was always seen as a food of the mines, and no fisherman could see himself down a mine. I don't know, to be honest.'

It was much the same with green being considered unlucky. This was a rock-solid rule (olive and mint aside), and yet no one was entirely sure of its origins, although there is strong evidence that in ancient mythology green is associated with illness and death.

The tradition has had an interesting offshoot, though. In old theatres the riggers were frequently men who had worked on the clippers and sailing vessels. They would assign one room for special equipment, a room that no one was allowed to enter, in effect a Green Room. This phrase has since passed into theatre parlance and, although there are a number of other suggestions for the origin of the phrase, this is my favourite and is therefore obviously the right one.

Looking at Black Head crouched ominously in the distance it dawned on me that should I happen to have a day when I didn't want to go to sea (and there would be many of those over the next few months), all I needed was a female priest walking among the boats of a morning, ideally dressed in green, holding a rabbit in one hand and eating a pasty with the other. I made a mental note to call a casting agency when I got back ashore.

But on a day like today, when the sun shone, the sea shimmered and *Razorbill*

'Never take a pasty onto a boat while you're in Cornwall. If you absolutely have to board a boat with one, make sure you stab it first'

proudly bore us to her hunting grounds, I simply would not have been anywhere else. I had the feeling that a great adventure and a great journey lay before me, epitomised by the wide sweep of an Atlantic horizon and the land mass that cast hard shadows on quiet coves.

'Here's some of my pots now,' said Nige, indicating a blue buoy which had appeared on the bow, nodding and pitching in the small choppy waves. 'I'll haul the string while you watch – piece of cake.'

'The pots were massive, like metal-framed coffins'

I was to learn a great deal about hauling pots in the next few weeks, but this initial impression lingered in the memory for some time. It still does to a degree. Nige eased off the throttle, hauled on the line attached to the buoy, strung it over the winch, started the winch, kept *Razorbill* in a straight line, manhandled each pot into the boat, opened it, extracted a few crabs and the occasional lobster, flipped startled undersized crustaceans back into the sea, placed bait in the pocket of each pot, closed the pot door, stacked the pot on deck and then repeated the process. The snag for me was that he appeared to do all of this at the same time, working various parts of the winch, boat, pots, lines and bait bags simultaneously with all four limbs, including making ample use of knees and elbows.

The fact that the boat was rocking gently in the swell at the time meant that he also had to slide elegantly from place to place as he worked. He looked like a man playing a very vigorous solo in a one-man-band outfit at a roller disco while collecting tickets and sweeping up behind him as he went.

The other alarming factor was that the pots were massive, like metal-framed coffins. I had rather imagined that they would be quaint little affairs, but these were great big killing machines. They appeared to weigh a great deal, not that Nige seemed to notice as he used the roll of the boat to perform a swift snatch and heave with each one, a clever combination of momentum and a stylish flick of the wrist seeing each land with a thump on the deck.

'S'cuse me, Mont,' he said, bustling past to once again push forward the throttle and reset the line of pots. This involved hurling out the marker buoy, then accelerating forward so the rope streamed over the side of the boat while Nige elegantly turned each pot over the side. The final buoy hurtled overboard to mark the end of the line and he looked at me with a smile, a small piece of kelp stuck to his cheek and not a bead of sweat on his brow.

'There we go. Easy, you'll pick it up in no time at all.' He gave a piratical wink and an encouraging smile. 'Right, back to Cadgwith, I'd say – it's getting a little bit late and we don't want the rest of the lads to worry, do we? That's it for today, but we'll get you doing some full strings of pots tomorrow. Great fun.'

As we motored home, I had ample time to reflect on what I had just witnessed. The entire process had taken about five minutes, but was such an effortless display of co-ordination and strength that I felt it really should have been set to music. What was particularly impressive was the way Nige had harnessed the movement of the boat and indeed the sea itself to lift and move the pots, although my admiration was accompanied by the appalling realisation that within a few short weeks I was supposed to be doing the entire thing on my own. It was a monstrous proposition and appeared to me to require a crew of at least five sturdy specialists and a bellowing supervisor.

Nige was to prove a great man for showing me the ropes, very much a 'hands-on' tutor, and as we approached the beach a few minutes later he eased off the engine cover with one foot. This exposed *Razorbill*'s clattering innards, at the back of which sat a small, bright red button. It was time for lesson number one.

'See that button there, Mont? You need to push it as we hit the beach – it cuts out the engine, you see, and stops us getting bits of seaweed in the water intake.'

I was delighted with this development, as it gave me a real job to do. What's more – I thought proudly – one that actually added a little bit of genuine value to my presence on the boat.

'Roger that, Nige,' I said, having suddenly come over all nautical. I crouched by the button, thumb poised over the top, as the beach approached and the engine thumped and rattled before me.

At the appointed moment I coolly hit the button. Sadly this meant leaning down and over the engine to make sure I hit it exactly right, and as I had decided that the moment of button depression would be on impact with the beach it meant we came to an abrupt halt. I, however, being in a somewhat vulnerable doubled-over position, carried on at a respectable three knots. And so my sole contribution to my first day's fishing was to pitch wordlessly, face first, into the engine block with only a brief pinwheeling of my left arm as a means of farewell to daylight and the deck. Nige, thank goodness, was looking up at the beach at the time and didn't glance

back down until I had extracted myself from wheezing pistons and floppy fan belts. I even managed an uncertain smile and vague oily thumbs up.

The apprenticeship would, it seemed, be short but never dull.

Nige hooked the cable from the winch onto *Razorbill*'s bow and we both jumped out to watch her waddle her way onto shore, dragged up the cove with considerable clattering from the winch hut.

I needed to settle into my accommodation properly, so after thanking Nige for my first experience of life on a fishing boat, I made my excuses and began to trudge back up the shingle. I had only gone a few yards when he called me back.

'Sorry, Mont, something I've just remembered.' He was rummaging furiously in the boat's locker as he spoke, so all I could see was the back of his head. 'I'll see you tomorrow, but before you leave I need to give you perhaps the most important piece of equipment for any fisherman.'

He continued to mutter to himself in the depths of the locker.

'I know it's here somewhere ... let me see. Aha, here we go.'

I could hardly wait. A sextant, perhaps? A marlin spike? A big knife? Some parachute flares?

He held out one hand. Cupped in the palm was an old alarm clock.

'On the beach ready to go at 6.30, then. Don't be late, there's a good lad.'

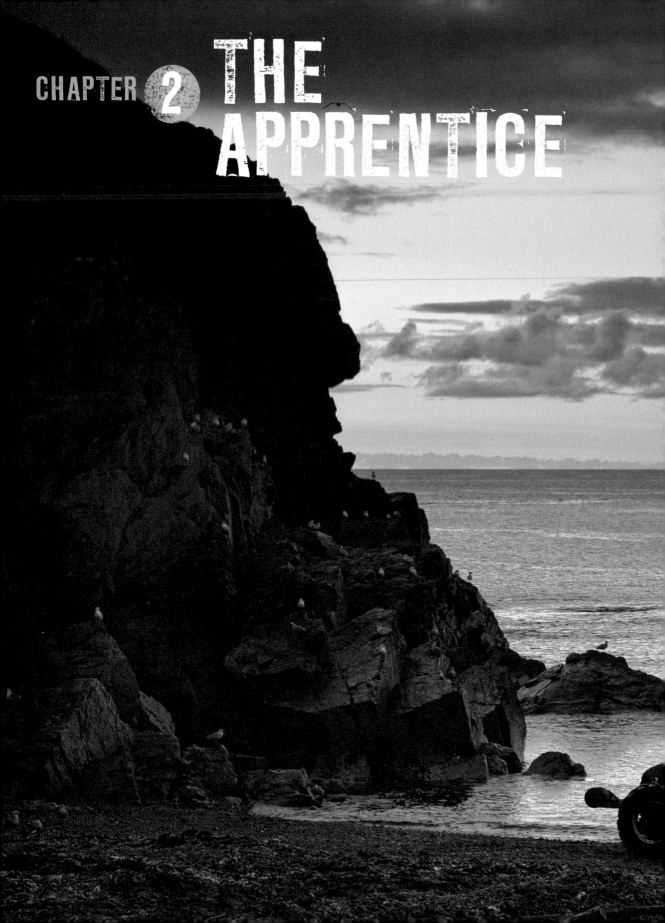

CHAPTER 2 THE APPRENTICE

Said alarm clock went off at the ungodly hour of 5.15 the next morning.

Not that it was entirely relevant to me as I'd spent most of the night staring with wide eyes at the ceiling, wondering what on earth I was doing here. I was gripped by genuine anxiety at the prospect of meeting the rest of the fishermen. How could I possibly match up to them? There is a brutality in the life of a fisherman, an authentic resilience and merciless work ethic that I had spent much of my life trying to emulate, but had never really matched. I knew my previous accomplishments and experience would all become irrelevant the moment I set foot on that beach. They would measure me as a fisherman, and accept or reject me on their own standards. The prospect was hideous, and as I ate my breakfast I looked miserably at a picture of my girlfriend and my dog many miles away in Bristol.

But every journey starts with a single step and mine was into my wellies in the porch. I then flapped and swished my way down the beach and into the soft light of dawn as the Cadgwith fleet stirred into life.

On Nigel's advice I had bought some new oilskins of the very brightest yellow. I already felt intensely self-conscious about the entire venture, a sensation not aided by my clumping passage towards the fleet, giving out a reflective light signature that could be seen from space. I looked like a colossal daffodil, the very newest and shiniest fisherman in Britain, a gigantic and pointless posh rubber duck.

It was a beautiful morning for the first real trip of my apprenticeship. As I rounded the corner into the cove, I was presented with a truly timeless scene as the fleet mobilised itself for the day's fishing. The tractor bustled between the vessels, crunching on the shingle and bellowing with effort as dark smoke spouted from its rusted exhaust. A platform behind it held boxes of bait and large blue tubs, which it delivered to each boat with a gentle whine of hydraulics. Moving quietly on the decks of the vessels were the skippers and crew members, tinkering with winches and peering at plotters, readying themselves for the day ahead. There was that special silence of a dawn that has emerged from the sea, punctuated only by the soft conversation of the men on the boats and the occasional burst of laughter. The walls of the cove echoed and amplified every sound, an enduring soundtrack to the theatre of the Cadgwith fleet preparing for the hunt.

There was just a beat, the merest hint of a pause in proceedings, as I walked round the corner. Not being entirely sure what I was supposed to wear, I had decided to stray on the cautious side and put on every single piece of waterproof clothing I possessed. This meant marching through the midst of the skippers and crew of the Cadgwith fleet wearing the aforementioned spanking new oilskins, the leggings of which were inconveniently hitched halfway up my shins as I hadn't quite figured out how to loosen the buckles.

'Morning, morning,' I said to various stilled figures as I walked towards *Razorbill*. One of them had a rolled-up cigarette suspended magically from his lower lip, his mouth hanging open in alarm as I approached. The men politely raised a hand or muttered a greeting in return as I passed. On reaching the end of the row of boats, and just before arriving

at *Razorbill*, I paused for a moment and looked behind me to take in the scene.

The fishermen who work here are, of course, in competition. Once their boats round the headland and charge towards the fishing grounds, it really is every man for himself. But here on the beach, co-operation is the name of the game, and it was only on observing more closely that the level of this co-operation became apparent. There was never a question asked, never a raised voice, and yet I was observing a scene of supreme co-ordination and teamwork. One by one the tractor pushed the fishing vessels down the beach, crewmen leaping between each one to take turns in driving, loading bait and lifting net boxes before vaulting aboard their own vessel as the stern hit the low surf.

'I was observing a scene of supreme coordination and teamwork'

Within minutes the beach was cleared, with each vessel heading to sea with the right crew, boxes of bait, a tank full of diesel and precisely the right kit for that day's fishing. I had arrived at 6.30 amid such bustle and industry that I could barely squeeze between the ranks of hulls. Fifteen minutes later and I was completing my walk towards *Razorbill* across empty shingle as the last boat disappeared round the corner of the cove. It was a wondrous sight, this group of men working entirely in harmony without a word between them, using choreography passed down the ages.

'Jesus Christ,' said Nige as he saw me for the first time, rather shattering the contemplative mood, 'where do you think

we're going today? We're only fishing round the corner, not the Grand Banks.'

He smiled broadly, shook my hand – a delightful little custom of his before each morning's fishing commenced – and I immediately began to shrug out of my oilskin top.

'That's better, Mont, I can actually see there's a man under there. Right, now the beach is clear, I'll give you a quick tour so you can see the nuts and bolts of how it all works. Let's start with the winch.'

If the boats are the heart of Cadgwith, then it is the winch that sets the rhythm, a great, snorting pulse housed in a weathered clapperboard box at the very top of the shore. A thick cable snakes away from the box, via a series of massive pulleys attached to a chain that lies across the top of the tideline. This is how the fleet is recovered at the end of each day's fishing, hauled up onto the shingle like waddling ducks.

Such is the importance of the winch that when someone new joins the fleet they have to be 'voted onto the winch' by the rest of the fishermen before they can commence operations. Fail to be part of this exclusive club, and you can't fish out of Cadgwith. The fishing operation is not only a near-perfect example of teamwork, but also a neat model of democracy.

As Nige showed me how to operate the winch – a case of turning a key, then flicking a lever – it seemed simple enough. It started with a clatter and a roar, then the cable drum hissed into life as I engaged the gears. The pulleys rattled and heaved, and the hook on the end of the wire began to carve a furrow in the sand as it moved sedately up the shore.

Little did I realise it at the time, but performing this same operation with a fishing boat attached to the end created the sort of pressure that made my brain short out. It's rather like hauling someone's mortgage, someone's entire livelihood, up a steep beach, with lots of other mortgages parked nearby and the entire operation controlled by a series of hand signals that are eminently easy to mix up in the heat of the moment. The first time I did it for real several days later, the winch hook appeared round the corner with all manner of interesting things attached to it. Bits of the tractor, a wellie boot, an annoyed fisherman, that sort of thing.

For now, though, I felt nothing but quiet confidence as Nige disappeared into the shed to turn the winch off.

'Good stuff, Mont, good stuff. Now, let's go and have a look at the tractor.'

The tractor is another essential tool for the modern Cadgwith fisherman, although it is regarded with a slight curl of the lip by the older, retired skippers. This is because its main function is to push the boats into the water at the start of the day, a job traditionally done by the men of the fleet working together. A number of fading images in the pub showed groups of men in oilskins leaning against the boats, faces puce with effort, striding in unison towards the water's edge. It looked marvellous, the epitome of this tight-knit community.

'Oh, it was a bloody awful way to start the day,' said Nige with commendable honesty when I asked him about it. 'You were knackered and you had wet feet before the day's fishing had even begun. Personally, I'm a big fan of the tractor.'

Imagine being asked to sit in a tractor on a steep and empty beach, being shown where all the levers, buttons, bells and whistles were, and then being told to go and do a series of handbrake turns, emergency stops and shingle-spewing

doughnuts. For the next half-hour passing tourists were treated to the sight of me vigorously pumping the clutch, brakes and accelerator, and conducting the sort of driving that should really be curtailed by a police marksman.

As it happened there was one boat left on the beach apart from *Razorbill*. Nige introduced me to the skipper and suggested that I might like to push his boat out. The skipper in question was John 'Mad Dog' Mitchell – an interesting character, universally acknowledged as one of the best fishermen on the beach and yet very much a man who kept his own counsel. He had a gimlet gaze that could bore a hole straight through you; as I gripped the wheel with sweaty palms and crunched the gears, I was forced to look at him as he stood in the wheelhouse, the two of us separated only by two panes of glass and a couple of yards. He stared back, daring me to get it wrong. Happily the launch went well, leaving his boat to putter out of the mouth of the cove, and a slight stain on the tractor seat.

'Good stuff, Mont,' said Nige, as I halted the tractor beside him. 'Right, let's give *Razorbill* a shove and get fishing.'

Nige's fishing grounds were essentially from the mouth of the cove all the way northeast to the tip of Black Head, which in the context of the Lizard Peninsula is a very civilised stretch of water indeed. Moments later we were rounding the corner of the cove, with *Razorbill* lifting her plump nose towards the dark mass of the headland in the distance. The seabed beneath us was a mix of sand and isolated reefs, ideal lobster and crab country. The buoys marking Nige's fishing gear bobbed at various points close to cliffs and craggy inlets along the coastline, and soon the first hove into view. I was desperately keen to assist in any

way I could, though my enthusiasm was more of a hindrance than a help: I leaped forward to grab the buoy and immediately wrapped the line the wrong way round the winch. I cranked the handle into gear and nearly got brained by the plastic ball beneath the main buoy. Nige chuckled and moved forward, slipping the handle out of gear, and showed me the correct way to loop the line over the hub of the winch.

And so the morning passed with Nige patiently instructing me on how to manoeuvre the pots into the boat, how to extract the crabs, how to re-bait the pots and how to re-lay them efficiently around interesting bits of broken seabed.

All the while the buckets and tubs in the bottom of the boat filled steadily with muscular edible crabs, the alien angles of spider crabs and the occasional dark form of a lobster, a sleek aristocrat amidst the hoi polloi of the crustacean peasantry around it. I was studying one of the tubs with interest when I heard Nige exclaim in delight from the bow as the latest pot came aboard.

'Now that's a lobster and half. There we go, Mont, catch a few of those and we'll be able to retire by October.'

I glanced round and saw him lift up a grand old man, a Chelsea pensioner in shining armour. The lobster probably weighed seven or eight pounds, and was pockmarked and scarred, with barnacles growing on its massive claws and sponges clumped on its carapace. It was a living piece of the seabed, a mobile reef that had become its own mini ecosystem over the many decades of its life.

'You know,' said Nige, as he turned the lobster in one hand, 'a few years ago I always kept these really big lobsters, but nowadays I tend to put them back. They're too big for one meal, and some say the flesh isn't as good as the younger ones, so they tend to get made into soup. That's no way for an old veteran like this to go, is it?'

He had a very good point indeed. There was every chance that Nige's father had caught that same lobster, as they can live to 70 or 80 years old, overcoming the most phenomenal odds in the process. It is one of the more remarkable life histories in the animal kingdom, and worthy of our respect and admiration.

'I glanced round and saw him lift up a grand old man, a Chelsea pensioner in shining armour'

Lobsters will mate in late summer, attracted to each other by the smell of their urine, incidentally – a similar system to that used in certain nightclubs in Plymouth, if my memory serves me correctly. The female has the ability to store sperm for several months and she will fertilise her eggs at the optimum time to maximise survival, generally in late spring of the next year. She will incubate about 20,000 eggs – or berries, as the fishermen call them – holding them under her tail for nine months using specially adapted edges to her shell. Such are the perils of life in the ocean that only one of those 20,000 will survive to maturity as a lobster that can breed and continue the cycle. We may have a romantic notion about our rocky shores and sandy bays, but they are places of ambush and decapitation for most marine life, very few of whom will make it through to sedate retirement.

The eggs are released into the water column by the female at night, lifting her tail and flapping it vigorously to send her brood on their way. After the eggs hatch, the larvae spend an action-packed three weeks drifting through the ocean, relying on the currents and tides to distribute them far and wide. This dissemination of offspring is key to the survival of any species, and lobster do it rather well, spreading quickly to access vast tracts of coastline and so preventing the young relying on a single region.

The larvae that survive this early stage settle on the seabed after a month or so and immediately dig in, creating a small burrow from which they will murder anything that happens to be wandering past. It's at this point that they really start to look like lobsters, with a shell consisting of 17 moving parts housing what is essentially a sociopath. They are tiny armoured nutcases, intent on scrapping and if possible eating anything that blunders into range. That includes other lobsters and a strict dietary regime that falls into the 'if it's smaller than me and alive I'm going to try to eat it' category.

After a year or so of this mayhem, the burrows collapse as the lobsters become larger and they venture out to scour the seabed at night like serial killers, spending the daylight hours under rocky ledges and in crevices. Their survival rate from this point on rises rapidly, and a good percentage will grow over the next five to seven years to produce eggs of their own, thus keeping the entire bloodthirsty cycle going.

Because the females greatly reduce their rate of feeding when carrying their eggs, they're rarely caught in pots. Even when they are, an initiative launched by the fishermen themselves means that they are generally returned, frequently with a V cut into their tails. This clearly identifies the lobster as a breeding female and means that she must be returned until the V grows out – a process that takes about three years. So there we have it: an elegant solution to the perpetual problem of how to identify those animals that can breed successfully and how to ensure their survival.

We soon had a fine haul of lobsters clicking and thrashing in the fish box at our feet, occasionally breaking off from their life or death throes to try to start a fight with their immediate neighbour. Nige picked them up one by one and slipped a rubber band over each claw.

'It's to stop them tearing each other apart, Mont,' he said. 'People often ask me on the beach why we do it. They always seem surprised when I say it's nothing to do with looking after the fisherman – it's all about the lobsters, really.'

It was soon time to head for home, and Nige leaned on *Razorbill*'s creaking tiller to turn her head towards Cadgwith, a journey she had made countless times. She surfed gleefully down the gathering waves, swishing her plump stern and lifting her prow, the cliffs protecting the cove thrown into stark relief as they grew ever closer.

'I bet you've had some exhilarating arrivals in the cove over the years, Nige,' I said as we crunched our way up the shingle, *Razorbill* leaning contentedly on her keel behind us after being pulled up the beach by the clattering winch. She looked entirely at ease, her day's work done and her skipper safely delivered to shore.

'Oh yes,' said Nige with a smile. 'Surfing certainly isn't a new fad in Cadgwith, let me tell you. I enjoy a bit of surfing myself every now and then, except my board weighs two tons and is eighteen feet long. Nothing like arriving at the beach doing a healthy ten knots with a big breaker up your backside, just polishes the day off nicely.' He winked and trudged on.

We parted with another handshake.

'Well done today, Mont, you made a few mistakes but it'll all come good soon enough. I'll see you tomorrow about 7.30 – bit of a lie in for you.' He gave another shout of laughter and turned to walk off with a half smile as he lifted his head to look at the village around him.

'My incompetence on Razorbill over the next months would have led many a man to set about me with a filleting knife'

Nige was a fisherman who had spanned the eras, starting out as a child making willow pots with the old men on the beach, graduating to running his own boat with crew and then downsizing to *Razorbill* before creating a portfolio of different activities that earned him a tidy sum when the boat was marooned on shore by the weather. He emanated the calm, grounded demeanour of a man who had seen a great deal. He had stared straight into the psychotic fury of hurricane-force storms, had seen endless tides wash over the shingle of Cadgwith beach, had watched whales and dolphins scull past the bow of his boat in the shadows of the immense cliffs that were the walls of his office, and sat idly at the head of the cove as tourists arrived in gleaming vehicles packed with bickering families.

It seemed to me that a lifetime of observation and a deep appreciation of his lot as a fisherman had created a profoundly contented man. The ever-present threats of his chosen profession had also spawned a rather philosophical approach to life, and so it seemed that for Nige every day held something special and rare. He had a keen sense of his own good fortune, of how when the dice of life were cast he had done rather well. My inexperience and incompetence on *Razorbill* over the next months would have led many a man to set about me with a filleting knife, yet at no point did Nige even raise his voice. I was to learn a great deal about fishing from him, but in the process I would learn considerably more about how to conduct myself through life in general.

I decided to spend the rest of the afternoon really getting to know the village. Every stone, crevice and dark nook in Cadgwith speaks of its maritime heritage. It's difficult to date its origins precisely, although it's almost certain that the first settlements here would have been created from a combination of driftwood, clay and branches from the thicket at the head of the valley – the village stirred into life as a combination of the earth and the ocean. Sometimes these origins are entirely obvious and sometimes they are a riddle that needs to be deciphered through careful forensic work, but if you look hard enough, pretty much every building, low rambling wall and twisting path can be traced back to the days of trade and fish. As further houses were built with timbers from shipwrecks washed ashore, slowly the village grew in much the same manner as countless others in sheltered coves around Cornwall, a county whose border is 80 per cent coastline.

It was in 1780 that Cadgwith's growth abruptly accelerated, driven by a family called Hawkins. These were the new landlords of the village, and they invested heavily in the pilchard industry. During this period substantial new buildings created a positively industrial scene at the head of the beach, as millions of pilchards were landed, processed and transported. I'd been told that the numbers were staggering and so set off to the old net store at the head of the cove where the larger catches were recorded.

'What a spectacle these great shoals must have been, vast dark shadows moving along the coast that represented great riches to the people of Cadgwith'

It was an easy matter to find the store – a substantial space above the winch shed – and I crept up a weathered set of wooden steps into the dark and musty fug of the rafters. Looped through the beams were the last of the great nets, immense and weighty like a cloud gravid with rain. It was this type of net that would be deployed by the entire fleet when a shoal of pilchards was spotted from above the cove, the cry of 'Hevva! hevva!' ringing out from the hut perched on the tip of the headland. This word – a call to battle for the entire village – derived from the ancient Cornish for swarming or flocking. What a spectacle these great shoals must have been, vast dark shadows moving along the coast, harried by dolphins and seabirds, a living storm front that represented great riches to the people of Cadgwith.

The men who called the village to battle when the shoals were sighted were known

as huers, and were important characters in the community. Carved into the wall by the old pilchard cellars is the inscription 'JFS 1908', a piece of graffiti that one John F Stephens created in an idle moment (or probably several idle moments; the letters are scored deep into the stone). He was known as one of the finest huers in the village; as such a prominent figure in the local economy I imagine he could write his name pretty much where he chose. It must have been quite a moment as that cry echoed around the cliff walls, galvanising the village with doors flung open and men running down the hill, boats being heaved down the shingle and crowds gathering on the Todden watching the fleet swoop towards the shoal.

Peering at the rafters above me I could make out the numbers of the catch, proudly inscribed as a testament to the prowess of the fleet and to a resource that must have seemed endless. 'Fish caught 1904. Nov 8th, 10th and 11th, 1,798,000 at 12/3d, 12/–, 10/– and 8/6 thousand' and a little further along '1908 September 4th 786,000, Sept 15th 227,000, 22nd 71,000, 24th, 25th 1,347,000.' There was an echo of another time in those words, a time when the community basked in annual harvests that bought prosperity for the rest of the year.

When the pilchards vanished, the fishing fleet remained, albeit in reduced numbers. In 1889 there were 50 fishermen working out of the cove; by 1976 that number had reduced to 26. By 1993 it had dropped further to only 13, and today a mere eight remain.

I ambled out of the loft and into the quiet of a late afternoon, the village hushed around me. The hill naturally took me towards the main wall above the beach, against which lay an old wooden bench known locally as the Stick. If the fishing

fleet is the heart of Cadgwith and the winch the pulse, then the Stick is its voice. This seemingly incongruous seat, resting against the rough stone of the old fish cellar, is surely one of the great debating spots in Cornwall (if not the entire world). It is said originally to have been the mast of the sailing vessel *Socoa*, wrecked in August 1906 on the rocks to the west. At the end of a day's fishing the men of the village would gather to sit on the Stick, leaning back against the wall, the stone of which still held the warmth of the day. They would fix their nets, they would peer out to sea, they would smoke, but above all they would talk.

It is a conversation with no end, no conclusion, and is handed down from one generation of Cadgwith fishermen to another. The fleet may embrace technology and modernity, but the conversation remains constant – the state of the tide, the location of the fish, and the weather. Always the weather.

As I walked past I noticed a figure sitting in the afternoon sun, back resting against the stones to harvest the last heat of the day. He was substantially built, barrel chested and bull necked, and glanced up as I approached.

'Hi,' he said, holding out one large paw to grip my hand in a firm shake of greeting. 'My name's Dom. It's very nice to meet you. You're working with Nige, aren't you? Good.'

He beckoned me closer, leaning forward conspiratorially.

'Now, the most important thing to remember about Nige is that he knows absolutely bugger all. As long as you keep that in mind, you'll be fine.' He sat back with a broad smile and looked very satisfied indeed.

The next morning I mentioned the conversation to Nige, who laughed uproariously.

'Yep, that's Dom,' he said, when he had calmed down a little. 'He's an animal, that bloke, does everything flat out and can lift an entire net bin on his own.' A full net bin weighs about 200 pounds and is about as awkward a shape as it's possible to lift single-handed. I made a hasty mental note never to fight Dom. Or even vaguely annoy him.

'It is a conversation with no conclusion handed down from one generation of Cadgwith fishermen to another'

It was on the Stick in the 1970s and 80s that Richard 'Buller' Arthur and his good friend Hartley would sing of an evening. It was nothing much at first, just a few songs at the end of a day, with Buller's deep bass combining beautifully with Hartley's tenor, the harmonies echoed and amplified by the wall behind them. But it was the start of something special: the tradition exists to this day, with the singers gathering every Friday night to bellow tunes in the Cadgwith Cove Inn.

The Cadgwith singers used to be made up entirely of members of the fleet, although nowadays there is a fair sprinkling of incomers. No one seems to mind, though, and it is quite appropriate given the nature of the songs that are sung. In their own way these are synonymous with the seafaring nature of the village, drawn from far shores and ancient traditions, entirely fitting for a place so dedicated to the limitless possibilities that sea travel presents. At one moment there will be a Negro spiritual, at the next a sea shanty, at the next a lament to a lost man. It is a sound to make the hairs on the back

Hot Pasties
Fresh Baked Now!

CADGWI
CORNWALL

BUCKETS

BULLER

of your neck stand up as it drifts through the windows of the pub and races out to sea.

Further into the heart of the village are the old cottages, most now given over as quaint holiday lets. Their transformation is only skin deep, though: they may have smart furniture and flat-screen televisions, but within there are mysterious cubby holes and lockers set in the walls, remnants of the days when smuggling was considered an entirely legitimate source of income for any coastal village in Cornwall. Many of the cottages were said to be connected by tunnels, escape routes for when the 'preventive men' came calling. These were the collectors of tax and duties, and were widely mistrusted. The South West Coast Path, at 640 miles one of the longest and most dramatic in Europe, was created so that the preventives could patrol the wild reaches of the Cornish cliffs and coves.

As I ambled past one of the cottages I could see the outline of a door set mysteriously in the first floor. Doors like this were said to be designed for a quick getaway from the press gangs (who 'energetically recruited' unwary civilians into the army or navy) and the preventive men. The fishermen would lower themselves into the darkness with the authorities in hot pursuit. Blinded by the red mist of the chase, the gangs would thunder through the door in their wake to briefly tread air before hitting the ground with the crackle of fractures and expletives.

By now it was pushing towards dusk and I turned back to the cove to find the tide lapping at the stern of the boats, the surface of the sea eerily calm. A large dark cleft in the rock wall was thrown into absolute darkness, looking endless and forbidding. This was a recognised feature, a crevice known as Miss Raven's Ogo,

which is simply the greatest name for anything ever. There is an explanation for the name itself – ogo being Cornish for cave and Miss Raven being one of the residents in Cadgwith in the 1890s. What she was doing in the cave, and why it was so important that it retains her name to this day, is lost in its shadows. As I turned for home it seemed to me that Cadgwith, this tiny village clinging to the edge of a ragged shore, was founded on the fruits of the sea and on the ever-present echo of those who had gone before. In its quiet cottages and timeless trails, it holds its secrets well.

* * *

That night Nige phoned to tell me that we wouldn't be fishing the next day ('Hooray,' said a tiny, inward, tired voice) and that I should meet him in his shed. So when I arrived at the beach the next morning it was well past seven o'clock and the fleet was long gone, leaving only a series of reptilian slithers in the shingle leading into the gentle surf. It looked as if a pack of amphibious predators had departed into the sea, leaving *Razorbill* alone on the beach, lost and vulnerable without the protection of the larger vessels around her.

The tide had completed its cycle since the previous evening and was well in, meaning that many of the gulls were off duty. They preferred low water, when great swathes of the shoreline were exposed and they could maraud from rock pool to rock pool, squabbling and shrieking like loitering hoodies. I glanced up to see them lined in a neat row on the ridge of the thatched roof of the pub. Nige had told me that this was one of the first things the fishermen of the cove checked in the morning. The gulls like to face into the wind, and their serried ranks offer a neat wind vane in an elevated position above the preternatural hush of the beach. If they are all facing out to sea, it means easterlies and a potentially difficult day's fishing.

This morning the wind was a mere whisper, nothing more than a gentle exhalation fading as it left the open spaces of the ocean and lost itself amongst the cottages. The sun had not yet had time to warm the beach, so the air remained deliciously cold and fresh, carrying just a hint of the night that had gone before. I inhaled extravagantly as I walked the last few yards to Nige's shed, taking in a heady mixture of damp undergrowth and sea air.

The shed sat in the midst of Cadgwith, a corrugated-iron monument to being a bloke, surrounded by thatched cottages and narrow cobbled lanes. Much of the exterior of the shed was barely distinguishable underneath twisting ivy, dark old nets, brightly coloured buoys and piles of old willow pots. When I pushed open the weathered door, resplendent with a jaunty image of a boat steaming determinedly towards the hinges, the dim interior revealed piles of fishing gear, heaps of old oilskins, jumbled stacks of exciting-looking tools and, right at the back, Nige himself. Light was provided by gaps in the roof, making it look as though the building had recently been strafed by a passing helicopter gunship. The door swung shut, pulled closed by a massive shark hook on a dangling lead weight.

'Welcome to the shed, Mont,' Nige said. 'Through there is the studio. That's where the great artist produces his masterpieces.'

Nige had realised at an early stage that there was potential income in expressing his love for the sea and for the fishing boats that were such a strong part of his identity. The most natural expression for him had been through painting, and the walls of the studio were covered in his work. All showed fishing boats ploughing through various sea states, from flat calm to mountainous waves. There was something about all the pictures that resonated with me, some common factor I couldn't quite pin down. Then it dawned on me. All of the vessels steamed from right to left. Nige saw my enquiring look.

'They're all going home, you see? I always like to paint them on their way back in, means that no one has been left out there.' He looked faintly abashed. 'If I painted one going the other way, for me that would mean that it was heading out to sea and I would always want to know if it had made it back to the harbour.' He paused for a moment, looking at the tattered carpet at his feet before giving a shake of his head. 'Silly old bugger. Anyway, coffee.'

We chatted amiably for a while in the studio, Nige sitting in an old winged armchair with a gas heater hissing beside him, creating a warm fug as the steam from our coffee – as strong and thick as tar – danced and twisted in the damp air. I sat on a bucket seat next to the wall, and after a rare pause asked him to sum up his life in the cove. He smiled, stared into the middle distance and sucked air through his teeth as he wrestled with a suitable response.

'A millionaire's lifestyle,' he finally said, 'without a millionaire's money.'

He chuckled, gathered his thoughts and then gestured towards a pile of brown sticks in the corner of the shed. They were tied together in dark, dense bundles, whip thin with deep brown bark.

'Withy pots,' he announced. 'Today we're going to make withy pots. It's the old way of fishing for crab and lobster, and there are very few people who remember how to make one properly. Happily for you I'm one of them, so I thought you could learn.'

'The shed sat in the midst of Cadgwith, a corrugated-iron monument to being a bloke'

The withy pot is a miracle of engineering, and I was delighted that I was going to get a chance to make one. Look at any fading picture of an old fishing village and chances are you will see stacks of pots crafted from willow, bound together entirely by natural materials. They were still in large-scale use until the 1950s, but then were swiftly replaced by metal and synthetic materials. These are far more robust and longer lasting, but have none of the beauty and elegance of their predecessors.

Nige began to bustle about the shed, placing a stand in the middle of the floor and dragging a pile of the willow from the corner.

'This was something the entire village did at one time. As kids we used to have to carry the bundles in from the fields. The farmers used to charge per bundle, so my dad just made the bundles massive so we'd pay less. Nearly bloody killed me.' He laughed, then bent to grab the first few sticks and sharpened the ends to place them into the stand.

He worked with astonishing dexterity, creating points of precisely the correct width and strength, before placing them in the stand, then weaving them together with smaller sticks from another bundle. He talked all the while, brought to life by the task, his hands twisting and bending of their own volition, deep memories embedded in the bones and sinews.

Once bound together at the neck, the main spars were then bent downwards towards the base of the stand, with smaller sticks being woven between them in an elegant spiral until the shape of the pot began to emerge. Even my untrained eye could see how immensely strong this structure would eventually become. Nige's hands, as powerful as steel clamps, wove the strands together, each complementing the other, every thin stick adding strength to the main spars that ran through the entire pot from mouth to base.

'When we chuck them in the sea, the water makes everything tighten up, so it really does become very secure. A good withy pot will last an entire season and catch many more lobsters than those metal things we all use nowadays.'

He paused for a moment, looking at the pot he had just created.

'You have to move with the times, of course, but it'll be a sad day when the last withy pot is made in Cornwall. It's a work of art, really, and comes entirely from the land to catch animals in the sea, which I quite like.' He glanced up from his work for the first time.

I had hardly spoken in the time it had taken Nige to make the pot, entirely content to watch him lose himself in a process that had been a feature of every fishing community in Britain for so many years.

'Did you enjoy making these when you were younger?' I asked.

He snorted. 'Bloody hell no, I hated it. The older fellas would give you a crack if you got it wrong, and of course there was no shortage of sharp sticks around to give you a poke.' He laughed again. 'It's only as I've got older that I've realised that a withy pot is a rather lovely thing. But then again you only appreciate certain things as you get that little bit older, don't you?'

He stood back from the completed pot, nodded in satisfaction, then looked over at me.

'Right, Mont, your go.'

The rest of the morning was punctuated by great gales of laughter, several cups of coffee and the eventual production of a monstrosity that wouldn't have captured an asthmatic prawn. My attempt at a pot was a wizened, misshapen affair, with an

arthritic bend at the top and weaving that unravelled at the merest touch. Nige eventually took over, noting the welts rising on my forehead where I had repeatedly whipped myself with errant willow sticks.

He looked at the result with pursed lips, scratching his beard with one thumb. He tried to think of something constructive to say, opened his mouth several times to speak and then thought better of it. He paced around the pot a few more times, peering at it from all angles.

'I think, Mont,' he said at last, 'that we should take that one down to the boat when it's dark, don't you?'

'Going to sea in a small fishing boat, hauling pots and setting nets is an uncompromising physical effort'

Over the next few days we would fish in earnest, with Nige a constant and patient mentor. I gradually began to understand the process of fishing and slowly came to terms with the demands of the job. Above all other factors was the superb work ethic of the men of Cadgwith. Going to sea in a small fishing boat, hauling pots and setting nets is an uncompromising physical effort and it seemed to me that much of the success of any small-boat fisherman was based on pure, simple graft. The relationship of cash to effort is direct and brutal. I had never worked so hard in my life.

Although the modern fisherman has the benefit of hydraulics, diesel engines and winches to haul the boat up the beach and tractors to ferry the catch to the cold store, there is still the simple, stark reality of spending a day on a factory floor that rolls and heaves beneath your feet. As an old South African fisherman noted to me on a filming trip many years ago, 'It's like spending the day on a horse – you're correcting and compensating all the time. You can be out there all day and do nothing, and yet you're exhausted when you come home.'

Of course for small-boat fishermen who specialise in catching crabs and lobsters, you have the additional factor of several hundred pots to shift each day. The lightest weighs in the region of 10 kilograms – most of them a lot more – and needs to be hoisted into the boat, manipulated so the door can be opened and the bait replenished, then stacked neatly on the deck before the next one arrives. This is all done at great speed as the world tilts alarmingly around you. And it's done all day, from early morning to – if you're lucky – early afternoon, and on many boats well beyond that.

A typical day involved a dawn start, but however early I got to the beach, Nige would invariably already be sitting on the Stick and glancing at his watch. After exchanging pleasantries, we would head to the cold store to collect a substantial tub of bait, drag it across the road, down the shingle and into the boat. With much grunting and heaving, we would lift this on board before getting the tractor to shove *Razorbill* into the shallows.

This was also the time when I would have a chance to chat to the other fishermen. One of the first I spoke to was John Tonkin, skipper of *Kingfisher 2*, a large, bright orange vessel. Just the same as every fisherman on the beach – and indeed around the UK – he had a nickname, which was nice and easy in his case: he was known by one and all as Tonks. A larger-than-life figure, Tonks, at 40-something, was the youngest skipper in Cadgwith and sported a baseball cap of staggering disrepair from which sprang errant tufts of dark hair. On one of the first mornings I walked onto the beach, I heard him shout across at me.

'Ere, Mont, you can't wear a bloody green hat, everyone knows that. Bad luck, it is. I'd whip that off if I were you.'

I sheepishly complied, feeling somehow that I'd let the lads down for the day. The next morning I turned up in a bright red woolly hat, to be greeted with a similar bellow from Tonks.

'Red? Red? Who dresses you in the morning for Christ's sake, your mum? Red is terribly bad luck – you'll need to lose that hat straight away.'

Once again I hastily stuffed it into my pocket before shuffling past, mumbling an apology. It was only later that I learned that red is perfectly acceptable and that Tonks was actually just enjoying himself with the new boy. He was a constant source of good humour and advice, and indeed during some of the darker moments in the future would come up and quietly tell me stories of his own early days and how hard he had had to work to overcome the myriad problems any small-boat skipper faced.

'You'll make it, Monts, don't you worry about that. Just sort your bloody headgear out – and while I'm on about it your jumper could use a bit of work, too.' By this he meant that my sleeves were too long. 'They'll snag on things, get wet with sea water and you'll end up with salt-water sores. Cut the bloody things off.'

He also advised me that the only way to do this was with a filleting knife in a stiff gale while actually wearing the jumper. If the sleeves matched in length after this process it was considered very poor form.

This type of robust exchange was to become very much part of the morning routine in the cove, although none of us could loiter for long. Having chatted briefly, there was always the need to get on with the job in hand as the dawn broke and the tide changed. Wishing each other good luck, we would climb aboard our respective boats and begin the trip to the fishing grounds.

'Nige and I would motor ahead in companionable silence, each alone with his thoughts as the sun began to warm the surface of the water'

This was always the best moment for me, with the wind in my face, *Razorbill* rocking beneath me, a ragged headland on the bow and the thump of the diesel driving us onward. Conversation always seemed strangely surplus to requirements at this stage of the day, and Nige and I would motor ahead in companionable silence, each alone with his thoughts as the sun began to warm the surface of the water over which we passed.

Typically we'd aim to haul six or seven strings, each consisting of five to seven pots, during the morning, with Nige working the winch and me hauling the pots over the side with considerable gurning and swearing. Nige seemed to enjoy this spectacle tremendously, never tiring of watching me wrestle a recalcitrant pot into a position where I could open the door to commence battle with its armoured occupant.

He could remove a large crab in an instant, whereas I would have to extract it by grabbing various portions of the carapace, all the while chattering to it like some desperate hostage negotiator. Nige's favourite moment of any particular day was the point when I miscalculated and managed to get pinched. By this stage we would be chatting away merrily, 'Well I must say, Nige, it's turned out beautifully, hasn't it? Lovely skies and a limpid sea. It's days like this that make it all seem...' – dramatic increase in volume to a bellowing – '...OW, OW, GET IT OFF, GET IT OFF.'

After working the pots, we would return to the cove with tubs of crab crammed on deck, clicking and crawling over one another. Another tub would be set aside for lobster, shining like great blue insects, the prime catch of any trip.

Just outside the cove we would lift a much larger pot marked by a brightly coloured buoy. This was the store pot where the crabs or lobsters would be kept until Nige's order book filled and they could be sold on. I would untie the lid and lift the crabs out of the tubs and into the pot, chatting away throughout:

'I always really enjoy this bit of the day, Nige, as it means we're at the end of fishing and nearly ho... OW, OW, OW, JESUS, RIGHT ON THE THUMB.' There would then be a considerable decrease in volume to a surly low mutter: 'Just because it happens all the time doesn't mean it's always funny, you know.'

And so the day's fishing would be concluded, with *Razorbill* turning the corner of the cove to nose onto the beach, with the village at its head to greet us.

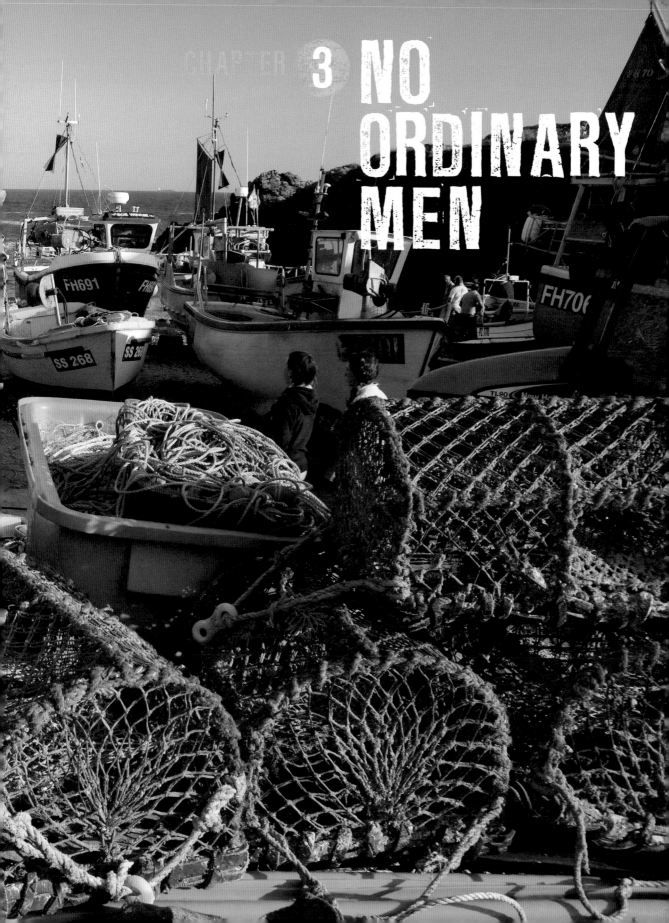

CHAPTER 3 NO ORDINARY MEN

As we readied the boat one particularly calm morning, Nige paused just before we shoved Razorbill into the water.

'I reckon you should have a go at putting out your own gear now, Mont,' he said, to my not inconsiderable alarm. 'I'll be watching, so don't worry if you make a few mistakes – we all had to learn at some point.'

We puttered out from the cove with me on the helm, scanning the shoreline looking for a likely spot that had a whiff of lobsters about it. I finally slowed the engine and nodded to Nige to indicate that this seemed to be as good a location as any. He simply raised one eyebrow, which I took to mean, 'What a remarkably perceptive choice, this boy's a natural.' It could also have meant, 'Good grief, what a drooling simpleton', of course, but being an optimistic type I decided it was probably the former.

I duly grunted and heaved my way through the deployment process, hopping and skipping over flailing ropes, trapping my thumb in the hinge of a pot, getting the order wrong and generally providing terrific entertainment for Nige. After all this considerable drama the final pot slithered overboard and the last buoy bobbed in the wake, leaving behind a clear deck and a breathless apprentice with a sore thumb and a glazed expression.

'Well done, Mont, well done. Told you you'd get the hang of it.' He looked like a proud dad at a school nativity play just after his boy had managed to blurt out the right line without wetting himself. I was delighted.

I was less delighted when we hauled the same string of pots a few days later and it was entirely empty. Nige smiled and tapped the side of his nose.

'You see, Mont, getting them in the water is just the first step. Now you need to start hunting! There's a bit more to fishing than chucking the gear over the side and hoping for the best.'

He was absolutely right. It was only after laying this first string of pots myself that I began to appreciate just how complex fishing is, and how many elements come into play when making the decision to place gear in a particular location. As we sculled along beneath the great cliffs of the Lizard, Nige was calculating and assessing hundreds of different factors.

What might appear to be a relatively innocuous exercise – making a short voyage in a small boat while randomly hurling a few pots over the side – is in reality a remarkable display of judgement and experience, honed over generations. On any given day the myriad decisions Nige makes – most of them entirely instinctive – will be the difference between a meagre catch and a good one. When the squalls come rolling in from a grey horizon, such decisions may also be the difference between returning with a bin full of crabs and not returning at all.

The first thing Nige must do is check the weather. This is generally done the night before, although there's also the final assessment done on the beach prior to departure. This phase – which the fishermen term the Winch House Blues – involves gathering next to the winch to peer up at the sky, mutter, look at the gulls, pace and then stomp off to the boat (or off home).

Cadgwith has its own set of rules about the weather, of course – it might be blissfully calm in the cove, but poke your nose out

'As we sculled along Nige was calculating and assessing hundreds of different factors'

towards Black Head or the Lizard Lighthouse and within minutes you might be battling vertiginous waves and slitting your eyes against driving rain. Easterly winds are a bit of a non-starter, as the waves they generate are funnelled by the cove, making launching tricky and landing impossible.

Then there is ground swell to think about. Generated far out at sea, this is a muscular wave that rears into a glassy wall many yards thick as it races down the gun barrel of the cove. It may be flat calm with clear skies, but such a swell can lock the fleet onto the beach, frustrated by a storm that may be thousands of miles away.

Once Nige has figured out all of this, he then becomes occupied with equipping the boat for the day. First there is the bait for the pots. This requires addressing a further series of questions, all of them crucial to the day ahead and indeed the ultimate financial success of the season.

How much bait? Too much and it may go to waste ('You might as well burn five-pound notes on the beach,' he said to me one day as I hurled excess fish to delighted flocks of gulls). Too little and you won't be able to re-bait the pots you've just hauled ('Starve the pot and you'll starve yourself,' he said as I glanced up from an empty bait container). Nige seemed to have a saying for every eventuality, although for some of my more excessive moments of imbecility he was occasionally struck dumb. I tried to look upon this as a small accomplishment on my part, as it took a fair amount to render Nige speechless.

And what type of bait to put in the pots? Crabs prefer fresh bait, whereas lobsters seem to prefer it either salted or rancid and carrying that special whiff of corruption and decay. This leads to one of the more delightful phases of any fishing trip – the sniffing of a fetid piece of suppurating fish

to make sure it is of sufficient vintage. This is done on a pitching deck while sweating in oilskins and is always something to look forward to. Various species seem to catch well – wrasse and mackerel work well for lobster, while ray and dogfish to do the trick for crab. Not the hind sections of dogfish, though – they don't seem to catch anything.

'Once again Nige consults an ancient mental chart based on many generations of local experience'

So that's the bait figured out; now Nige needs to address the state of the tide. It's not enough just to have a look at the tide tables, he needs to leaf through the mental notes of many, many years of previous fishing trips and figure out which particular bays will be at the right state of the tide to set and haul the gear. This changes as the boat moves along the coast and as the tide ebbs and floods along the length of the Lizard. Misjudge this and you'll be hauling against a flood tide, an undersea river that is pulling everything in the wrong direction and may even drive your vessel under the surface if your gear comes fast on a rock on the seabed below.

So that's weather, bait and tides sorted. Now there's the ground on which to set the pots. Get the substrate wrong and you'll catch nothing, or the wrong thing. Once again Nige consults an ancient mental chart based on many generations of local experience, directing him to certain sites where rocks meet sand or where steep walls end in great jumbled piles of boulders. This precious undersea chart can only be drawn through the work of those gone before, long before the dawn of echo sounders and side-scan sonars.

Having figured out where to go and when to go there, he then needs to think about the movements and feeding activity of the prey. Sometimes the crabs and lobsters move overnight and sometimes they don't. Sometimes they feed and sometimes they don't. There is a series of environmental triggers and clues – water temperature, time of season, wave action – that a fisherman needs to learn in order to catch effectively. Sometimes everything will seem absolutely spot on, but the absence of only one of a hundred factors will mean empty pots and a wasted day.

'It struck me what a sad day it will be when we lose the extraordinary piece of software that is Nige's brain'

While shooting and recovering fishing gear, any vessel's ability to manoeuvre is limited. Shackled to the sea floor, it cannot respond swiftly to changes in conditions or sudden events. And it's here that Nige must really switch on, constantly scanning and assessing the conditions around him. It might be an unpredictable shift in the wind, a swirling eddy as a wave hisses backward from a rock face, or another vessel appearing out of the gloom on a collision course. Fail to monitor your surroundings and you court catastrophe.

And at last comes the final factor – luck. Fishermen are notoriously superstitious, and it's no wonder. No matter how much knowledge has gone before and how experienced a particular skipper may be, occasionally the ocean will offer up a surprise that tilts all preconceived notions entirely on their axis. These are the days when the conditions are all wrong and yet the pots heave with clicking lobsters, when the weather looks appalling and yet abruptly clears to allow a superb day's fishing. However much we may think we know about the sea, she still holds a great many secrets in echoing vaults, occasionally dropping her guard to offer something that defies reasonable expectations.

On these days the fishermen will think about what they have done differently – putting one glove on before another, turning their boat a particular way out of the cove, wearing a certain hat – and they will repeat that habit from that point on as though appeasing the gods of the sea. When life is so very uncertain in the hunting grounds out on the horizon, why tempt fate?

As we headed back to shore after my first fruitless deployment of pots, it struck me what a sad day it will be when we lose the extraordinary piece of software that is Nige's brain. All that knowledge, all that experience of tide, wind and wave, will be gone. Lose our fishermen and we become a nation tied to the land, with the secrets and treasures of our shallows vanishing on the next tide.

* * *

As the three weeks of my apprenticeship slowly passed on *Razorbill* – hauling only 48 pots a day, I hasten to add – I noticed my body subtly begin to change. I grew leaner, with excess fat burning away from my midriff like some sort of eco-fuel, while my arms became corded and burned brown by the sun. My core strength improved dramatically as I spent each day twisting and turning on slightly bent knees, holding a weight at the level of my navel. It is no coincidence that Cornwall has fielded some of the finest scrum halves in rugby

history. The slow walk up the shingle at the end of the day took place on weary limbs, and I would slump on the sofa at home completely spent.

Although working on *Razorbill* was very genteel indeed compared to crewing on the larger boats in Cadgwith, a real exposure to the savage workload of a British fisherman came in the form of an invitation from a boat based outside the cove.

> 'The athleticism and endurance of the fishermen was a revelation to me, a painful glimpse into another world where the rules of graft and toil were set in stone'

Word of my foray into the world of fishing had spread among the local communities and I was invited onto *Harvester*, a really substantial potting vessel working out of the nearby port of Mylor. A solid twin-hulled platform some 50 feet in length, she was rumoured to have in the region of 2,000 pots out fishing at any one time. This number was somewhat vague, due to the inherent problems of trying to get a straight answer from any fisherman about the scale of his particular operation. Nige was quick to recommend that I accept the invitation, as it would show me a very different scale of fishing and perhaps provide a bit of intelligence as to just how many pots *Harvester* was using.

'Besides which, it'll be good for you, Mont,' he said as we sipped coffee in the shed. 'Might even get a proper day's work out of you. Imagine that.' He shook his head in wonder and raised a laconic eyebrow at the thought.

If even Nige was describing it as a proper day's work then the prospect was fairly horrifying, but it was important that I accept the invitation. A day on *Harvester* would give me a fascinating glimpse into our latter-day obsession with catching crabs in larger and larger quantities.

Although there is no quota for catching crabs in the UK, there is a requirement for a licence and a size limit for what is caught. In fact the majority of crabs that climb into the pots are undersized, so about 60 to 80 per cent are thrown back unharmed. This means they essentially get overnight accommodation with some mates, a buffet and a free flight as they are frisbeed back overboard. Some seem completely addicted to it and are caught again and again.

As with lobsters, hen crabs don't feed when they're carrying eggs – up to three million at a time, by the way – so they don't (as a rule) enter the pots. Even when they do the fishermen tend to throw them back. They also return crabs that are diseased and any that are soft shelled, as these are full of water and not good for eating. So we seem to have a beautifully sustainable industry, essentially nurturing the adolescents of the target species and ensuring the survival of the breeding females.

And then there is the low impact of the pots themselves. They are dropped onto the sea floor, generally stay in one place (although they can very occasionally be dragged by strong currents or unexpected storms) and are then hauled straight back to the surface. There's no dragging or towing, no cutting swathes through soft substrates or across delicate reefs. They just sit there, quietly catching freeloading crabs.

But if there is a way of messing up a rather elegant and effective fishing system, we humans will be sure to find it. In the 1980s a new type of potting vessel emerged in Brittany, the so-called Super Crabber. These monster boats could spend weeks at sea, had holding tanks on board that could contain tens of thousands of crabs and fished using thousands of pots.

Soon these Super Crabbers were replicated in the British fleet, along with a great many medium-sized boats that could stay at sea for several days and fished using over a thousand pots. In 1978 25,000 tonnes of crab were caught by the European fleet as a whole (which essentially means the French, Norwegians, Irish and British). In 2007 it was up to 60,000 tonnes. For the last decade the British have caught over half of this total, 90 per cent of it with these new, larger vessels. This has flooded the market and depressed the price, so everyone is fishing hard to catch lots and lots of crabs, simply in order to cover their costs. This in turn floods the market with crab, which depresses the price, which means everyone has to catch more crabs. And so it goes on until someone, somewhere does something about it.

Harvester was only a medium-sized crabber, despite her 2,000 pots. This doesn't suggest that she was a renegade vessel, of course; it is simply a reflection of the modern crabbing fleet.

And that's another problem. The Super Crabbers, the medium-sized crabbers and the smaller inshore fleet can't seem to agree on anything. There's no single voice for the fleet as a whole, although if there are three things they all agree on (and they're probably the only three) it's that the EU hasn't got a clue, the British Government are soft-palmed saboteurs destroying their industry, and the conservation lobby should butt out and get on with knitting some yoghurt sweaters.

This flooding of the market with crab, and the tough economic climate that has ensued, mean that of the 3,700 licences issued to boats to fish for crab, 20 per cent are not being used. The snag here is that should legislation finally be agreed between the warring factions within and outside the fishing industry, it would almost certainly result in either a quota system or a limit to the number of pots a vessel can deploy. This in turn would decrease the number of crabs caught (hooray), which would raise the price (hooray), which would almost certainly mean that those 20 per cent of vessels not fishing for crab at present would start again (boo). This would mean more crab on the market, decreasing the price and causing everyone to catch more to make ends meet. And so the cycle would begin again.

That's not to say that crabbing at its present level isn't sustainable – it may well be. But such is the speed of development of technology and the increase in the size of vessels that the scientific community has been caught somewhat on the hop. Just how many crabs are there out in the deeper water off the edge of Britain? How far do they move? How successful is their breeding strategy? How many can be taken before populations crash? No one really knows at present, although frantic efforts are being made to answer precisely those questions.

What is unequivocal is that the traditional smaller vessels of the inshore fleet are the innocent party here. They catch a tiny percentage of the total crab on the market, deploying a few hundred pots in a way that has changed little since their forefathers were hauling withy pots hand over hand. The fishing fleet at Cadgwith can get off the beach on only about 150 days a year, so the weather is their quota system, and the size and range of their vessels limit their fishing capacity.

As Nige and I hauled our pots from the same grounds that had been fished by his father and the many generations of Cadgwith men before him, there were storm clouds gathering on the horizon that threatened the entire fleet as never before. The swirling isobars of industrial-scale potting, of improving technology, of a market flooded with crab and lobster, and of an industry that cannot agree a common strategy – all of these meant that the future of the vessels that are the essence of Cadgwith Cove was suddenly more uncertain than ever.

* * *

The only snag in accepting the offer to work on *Harvester* was that it meant a 5 a.m. start, and what's more Mylor was an hour's drive away.

I was awoken by my alarm going off at 3.45, allowing me an entertaining 15 minutes of stumbling around the bedroom with my jumper on backwards, one eye gummed shut and a general sense of impending doom at the day ahead. Miraculously the jumper, the eye and the doom were all dealt with, so I began my nocturnal drive to the port pretty much on time.

The day that followed was beyond imagining. In the company of the crew – Henry, Jamie, Dusty and Jurgen – I helped work 600 pots. You could not have found a more decent, friendly, enthusiastic bunch of people on a boat. They were extremely kind to me all day (particularly as I spent much of it throwing up over the port rail – 'You checking the wheels?' asked Dusty as he wandered past at one point). And yet these were men of iron, relentless machines working to an extraordinary level of intensity. At the end of the day I asked the skipper's son Jamie – a particularly friendly, genial character – if he had much of a home life.

'Of course,' he said, 'happily married with three kids, actually. I'll get home at about 7 p.m. or so, play with the kids, do a bit of reading, generally crash out at about eleven, then up again at 4 a.m. to get ready for the next shift.'

He went on to say that this routine took place six days a week throughout the year.

'We very rarely lose a day to bad weather as we're slightly larger than the other crabbers working this stretch of coast. It's a great life, you know – who'd be in an office when you can do this?'

At that precise moment I happened to be skidding past him on deck at a vertiginous angle, eyes wide in alarm, holding a pot at waist height, with dried vomit on my oilskins and the thrashing waters at the open stern approaching at a considerable rate. I somehow arrested my progress, leaned again on the rail and thought longingly of quiet desks, carpets, water coolers and potted plants.

There was, however, no denying the intense bonds that united the team on board, forged in many a storm and brutal working shift.

Dusty told me of a member of the crew who had worked with them several years previously. A powerful, rather quiet man, he had initially struggled to fit in, eventually settling to the position of placing the baits in the pots. One day he approached Dusty and shyly asked what the rest of the crew thought of him.

'We all think you're fine,' said a slightly surprised Dusty, adding in moment of inspiration, 'in fact I'd go so far as to say you're now a complete master baiter.'

'A complete master baiter!' said the new man, 'What, really? A total master baiter? That's terrific!'

He spent that evening in the pub telling all and sundry of his new status, as proud as punch but perhaps slightly baffled by the warm smiles that greeted news of his promotion.

Jamie and rest of the crew laughed and shook their heads as Dusty recounted the story, all the while lifting pots, sorting crabs and working at a rate that would destroy most men very swiftly indeed. They seemed entirely content, totally at ease in their surroundings, with bedlam and the sounding depths of a great ocean only a hull's width away.

We returned to Mylor at six in the evening, having worked an 11-hour shift. As I thanked the crew and stumbled off the boat (fighting the urge to drop to my knees and kiss the concrete of the quay like the Pope stepping off an aircraft), Jamie walked up behind me and clapped me mightily on the shoulder.

'Well done, that man,' he said with the broadest of smiles. 'By the end there you almost looked like a crabber. We'll make a fisherman of you yet.'

I glanced up at the crew as they too disembarked and saw something I had not noticed before. It was present in the Cadgwith men as well, something in their demeanour that celebrated their independence and their way of life, as well as their defiance of the odds on a daily basis. No matter how friendly and jocular their approach, there is a look in their eyes and in their body language that says that they are not ordinary men. They are fishermen.

The men who skipper and crew boats large and small, who make forays beyond the safety of quiet coves and sunlit shallows, are the latest in an extraordinary breed. They are the final hunters of our island, a proud clan who pursue and catch wild animals for our food, the last still standing in a line that stretches to our distant ancestors. Again and again I met fishermen who were intensely proud of their profession, who would not exchange the hardships, the danger and the long hours for any other job on earth. They would look out onto a grey, flecked sea as it roared and heaved against dark granite cliffs, and they would smile. Day by day I was learning a little more about what it would take to become one of their number.

There are dark rumours that this present generation of fishermen may be our last. With the average age of a UK fisherman being 49, and very little sign of enthusiasm in the next generation to pick up the lines and the pots, these may well be the final few decades that we see large numbers of small fishing boats off our coast. It is not just the apathy of the Xbox generation, nor the price of fuel and the diminishing fish stocks. The fishermen face something much more insidious. I would frequently look on baffled as Nige tipped plump cod back overboard, muttering darkly about the impenetrable bureaucracy involved in being a modern fisherman.

'Wonder what my old man would have made of it?' he said one day, watching a dead cod twist down through the water column to eventually vanish into the gloom. 'All this business of rules and regulations would have driven him quite mad, I think.'

What I was witnessing was the end point of a vast array of factors, a series of ecological, technological, political and legislative events that have evolved and mutated over time to produce a wanton waste of a dwindling resource. Today we see an industry hog-tied with utterly impenetrable legislation, fish stocks under greater pressure than ever before and bewildered men throwing their catch back into the sea. This relatively recent

'There is a look in their eyes and in their body language that says that they are not ordinary men. They are fishermen'

development is creating an intractable division between those who undertake the fishing and those who attempt to control their catches. To understand the creation of this positive blizzard of red tape, it is necessary to delve a little into the history not only of our fishing fleet, but also of our fish stocks, our marine environment and indeed of our nation itself.

As an island race, we have always considered fishing to be an integral part of our culture. The once simple artisanal model of a small fishing fleet supporting a local community very quickly faded as larger-scale fishing became the norm, with the arrival of the steam engine in the early 20th century. In 1900 only 3 per cent of the 700-odd herring drifters in England and Wales had steam power; a mere 15 years later that figure had risen to 80 per cent. This development saw a sudden increase in the power and range of fishing boats.

Fish processing and the logistics of distribution improved dramatically in the same period, and soon traditional fishing grounds such as the North Sea were experiencing an unprecedented level of exploitation. As stocks were depleted, the industry responded with a simple maxim – fish further away in untapped regions.

And so technology began to play an important role, with ever larger vessels being built that could fish hundreds of miles away, much more efficiently and for longer periods. The hardships endured by the Arctic fishing fleets working out of Hull, braving polar waters for vast catches, have long since passed into fishing folklore. Closer to home fish such as herring saw battle lines drawn between the European nations, as in the 1930s Germany and Norway developed purse seines and mid-water trawls that enabled them to fish on a larger scale and further

afield while Britain lagged behind with outdated methods.

In Iceland, the establishment of a 12-mile fishing exclusion zone in 1958, and then a 50-mile one in 1972, saw the eruption of the Cod Wars, with fishing vessels from Britain and Iceland cutting each other's gear, ramming one another and being supported by warships in a stand-off that very nearly developed into a full-blown conflict. As fish stocks dwindled and national fleets began to scour the world's oceans for their catch, so coastal fishing limits were disputed and historical rights examined: tension and mistrust were the order of the day.

> 'Fish stocks dwindled and national fleets began to scour the world's oceans for their catch'

Amid all this uncertainty, the fishing grounds close to home were in real trouble, facing immense pressure from a European fleet that had more power, range and fishing ability than ever before. Some fisheries collapsed completely – a good example being the herring on Britain's eastern seaboard – ending thousands of years of sustained fishing efforts. Some limited legislation did exist, with Britain having led the way with the Sea-Fishing Industry Act in 1933, which established minimum net-mesh size and fish-size limits. Nonetheless the combined efforts of boats from other nations, and the vast capacity and range of the new fleets, meant that many European fisheries faced the distinct possibility of being entirely fished out. It was plain that some sort of collective action was required and – just in the nick of time, it seemed – galloping over the horizon came the EEC.

In 1957 six nations had formed the European Economic Community, a new dawn in international co-operation with the sole aim of ultimately creating a financial colossus that would dominate world markets. In the early 1970s, after a great deal of political huffing and puffing, the United Kingdom finally joined this multilingual, multicultural party. The concept was noble, the assets awesome and the reality an administrative nightmare. Among the common assets to be pooled were the European fish stocks, with control being ceded to Brussels under the Common Fisheries Policy. This was a rare opportunity to monitor traditional fishing grounds, as well as regulating European fishing activity in vast tracts of ocean that were suffering from hundreds of years of over-exploitation.

Of course no one wanted to see fish stocks eradicated – not the legislators, not the scientific community and certainly not the fishermen. It seemed, however, that the behemoth that was the EEC was such a mass of contradictory information and delicate political sensibilities that very few coherent strategies emerged. One that did eventually stagger through the system was quotas.

This noble effort to control the depletion of key fish stocks appeared in 1997. The principle was simple enough – allocate each vessel a limited amount of each species to catch. As long as this limit was below the level required to maintain healthy stocks, surely the European fishing grounds could begin to recover. Amid much back slapping and *holas* the legislation was passed. But there were three main flaws.

The first is that fishing gear tends to be fairly indiscriminate. Try as they might to avoid netting non-quota species, the fishermen kept catching what was around their boat at the time. The nets couldn't distinguish between a legal haddock and an illegal cod. No one thought to mention the new rules to the fish either, so they continued to swim into the wrong nets even when they were not supposed to. So when a cod ended up in the wrong net, being hauled into the wrong boat, it duly died, only to be chucked back into the sea by a singularly baffled and annoyed fisherman.

Most fish hauled from deep water will die – a study in 1984 noted that of the 40 million whiting caught and discarded that year, none survived. A further study in 1987 in the Torres Straits between Australia and New Guinea saw a 98 per cent mortality rate in finfish that were caught in trawls and thrown back. The journey to the surface alone might not be fatal, but the additional impact of being crushed in the net and then sorted on deck for several minutes resulted in what a 1994 UN Food and Agriculture report called a 'very low' survival rate. The conservation measure of returning what is essentially a corpse to the sea has – obviously – limited effect in improving stocks. But the quota system insists that they are thrown back – in vast, vast quantities.

The second flaw was that quota allocation proved to be over-generous, causing fishing pressure in some areas to actually increase. In the North Sea alone in 1970 only 10 per cent of fisheries were considered to be over-exploited. By 2000 that had risen to 50 per cent. Quota allocation was also rather lopsided, tending to favour the larger boats. Even today the small-boat fleet (which makes up 80 per cent of all types of fishing boat around the UK) has only 3 per cent of the quota despite having 8 per cent of our fishing capacity.

The third flaw was that quotas were not controlled tightly enough. Although the original quota was allocated to vessels that were actively fishing, if one of those vessels subsequently went out of business it kept its quota. This led to the not unreasonable step of fishermen selling their quota in much the same way as they would sell an engine or a net – to the highest bidder. But there was nothing to say that the bidder had to come from within the fishing industry. This led to fishing quotas becoming nothing more than assets to be traded on the financial markets, and to the development of a much maligned type of fisherman called a 'slipper skipper'.

This character spends much, if not all, of his time tied up alongside the quay and makes his money by trading entirely in quota he has purchased from other skippers. This in turn leads to someone like Nige bobbing around off Black Head, desperately trying to purchase quotas so he can keep enough of his catch to make a living, and yet in doing so lining the pockets of a fisherman – or indeed a businessman – many miles away who will release only enough quotas to make a profit for himself.

The utter absurdity of this situation was, happily, recognised by the British Government, who commissioned a Select Committee report in 2010. The committee set out with commendable gusto to reveal the entire grubby business for what it was. But they couldn't find out where all the quotas were because no one would tell them. No one would tell them because – alarmingly – no one really knew.

Since 1997 such had been the buying and selling of quotas that the Department of the Environment, Fisheries and Rural Affairs (DEFRA) had lost track of it all. The list of names of those who could grant permission for our fishermen to catch some fish had been lost. The Select Committee did manage to ascertain that some quotas were held by a Premier League football club.

'Of course no one wanted to see fish stocks eradicated – not the legislators, not the scientific community and certainly not the fishermen'

Anne McIntosh, the head of the committee, finally remarked in a BBC interview, 'We must have a register to determine who exactly owns the UK's fish quota.'

This calamity has grown worse over time, spawned by a combination of yawning cultural divides, an impossibly complex legislative matrix and simple greed. It has resulted in fishermen – good men from proud fishing families – tipping their catch overboard and watching their livelihood twist and spin into the depths.

It is also a something of an environmental tragedy. Who would have thought that today's fishermen, seeking out the remnants of the once great shoals of yesteryear, would be reduced to catching fish and then throwing their dead bodies back? And the really heart-breaking part of all this is that in many cases the quota that would permit them to keep the fish exists, but it's either being withheld for financial gain or is simply too expensive for a small-boat fisherman to buy.

We are witnessing one of the great cultural scandals of our generation – the eradication of a traditional, sustainable industry, the waste of a dwindling natural

'His boat was 18 feet long, his armoury some lobster pots and a few nets. His crew consisted of a blundering oaf on work experience' resource and the squandering of a precious foodstuff in a world starved of protein.

There are many suggestions as to how the future of the fishing fleets can be assured. Perhaps one of the simplest would be to recall all of the UK's quota and to return it where it belongs – to the fishermen.

I thought of Nige and how fishing had been his entire life. Although he had previously been involved in activities as diverse as crewing on larger boats and setting static nets on a not inconsiderable scale, his operation nowadays was simplicity itself. His boat was 18 feet long, his armoury some lobster pots and a few nets. His crew consisted of a blundering oaf on work experience and his fishing grounds were meticulously planned to be within a 40-minute steam of the Cadgwith Cove Inn.

I asked him about modern legislation as we prepared the boat one cold, clear morning, causing him to pause in his work and clear his throat. He seemed to be gathering his thoughts before picking his words, and although gathering and picking were very much Nige's forte, in this case he was really taking his time.

'Well, Mont, it's like this. I got a bit of paper the other day from some bloke in an office in London telling me that I'm not allowed to catch sprat in Iceland. From what I understand, Iceland is just round from the Lizard. It's easy, just keep Mullion to starboard, then motor dead ahead for 600 miles. Even with your navigation we'd struggle to miss a marker buoy by that much.' He smiled wearily, shaking his head and staring at the surf as it flopped lazily onto the beach.

'Over the last four or five years it's become an absolute nonsense. There are so many rules and regulations, and they change so often, that we really don't have the faintest idea what we're supposed to be doing next.

It's criminal really, and it's making good men – fishermen I've known all my life – despair. The whole thing...' and here he paused, struggling for the right words, 'is a right lash-up. That's what I think, anyway.'

The root of the problem appears to be the complex hierarchy that attempts to control the activities of British fishermen. Essentially the management of fisheries in the United Kingdom is governed first by EU legislation, then by national policy as set by the British Government and then by local bylaws. These in turn are governed by the Sea Fisheries Committee (SFC), which has recently become the Inshore Fisheries and Conservation Authorities (IFCA).

And there's more. The licences for fishing are issued and managed by the Marine Management Organisation (MMO), although at present no more are being issued. Just to add to the mix, there are considerable regional differences in local bylaws, and layered on top of everything else are historical rights. These are afforded to locations where fishing has always taken place, and mean – just by way of an example – that French trawlers can come to within six miles of the British coast, even though territorial waters extend to 12 miles.

And so when Nige putters out of Cadgwith in *Razorbill* of a morning, he has the EU, DEFRA, IFCA and the MMO keeping a beady eye on what he's up to. It's not surprising that he looks faintly bewildered on occasion.

* * *

A temperate shore is entirely beholden to the seasons, shifting from tranquil, crystal-clear conditions in the spring and summer months to a place of flecked violence and elemental power in the winter. As the conditions alter, so the marine life

responds, following timeless trails and patterns of behaviour that have dictated the movements of the men who hunt them. The latest major event – eagerly anticipated by the fishermen – was a great, clicking, armoured invasion, an elaborately spined army high-stepping its way towards the land from where it had overwintered in deeper water. The spider crabs had arrived.

This seasonal fishing was something of an annual highlight for Nige, being ideally suited to the small inshore fishing fleet. The larger boats with all their might can never really accomplish this kind of fishing, as it is altogether too close to shore and too labour intensive. Although in Britain we regard spider crabs as inedible and sinister (they are neither), on the Continent they go quietly mad for them. And so they should – a spider crab arriving at the table is a cause for celebration, a giant red monster stuffed with delicious sweet meat that has to be removed using pliers and Gallic swear words. What a great way to eat. Why on earth don't we do it?

Nige met me with the customary hand-shake one overcast morning and, glancing up at the sky, announced that today would be a good day to go after the spiders.

'We tend to use nets for them, Mont, as they move across the sea floor and get tangled up. Give me a hand with the net box and we'll be on our way.'

The net box in question was – needless to say – very heavy. I dragged it across the shingle, and one of the other skippers ambled over to help, chatting amiably all the while. This was just the beginning of the great aid to conversation that is netting for spider crab, something I was to discover as the day progressed.

We motored around the corner of the headland with me on the tiller and Nige indicating our course with a slight lift of the chin. He looked thoughtful, quietly leafing through that age-old mental manual as the day stretched before him.

It was a grey morning, with the surface of the sea slightly choppy, and it took several minutes' motoring close to the coast before we passed the old serpentine works in Poltesco Bay. The ruins of the factory were long overgrown, being quietly reclaimed by the land to become shadows on a map, the fading echo of a once bustling industry.

'We'll put the net down a few hundred yards off Kennack Sands,' Nige said. 'The tides are fairly good for a couple of days and I'm sure the crabs will be moving with these conditions. I've got a net already set just off Carrick Luz, so we can dart up there afterwards and see what we've caught, if you like.'

Setting the net was surprisingly easy, involving Nige simply steaming ahead while I lobbed a weight over the side on the given signal. This dragged the remainder of the net overboard as we motored along, leaving it to settle on the sea floor in a billowing, deadly curtain. The mesh was huge, several inches wide, allowing all but the most suicidal fish to swim through, and yet entangling the spider crabs as they trundled along the sand. This system works very well indeed, thanks to a flaw in spider crab design that means their shell is a series of sharp spikes and pointy projections. This is fine when they want to fend off predators, but is a distinct hindrance when they come across Nige and his nets.

We quickly finished deploying the net, the ends of which were marked – rather incongruously – by two cheap footballs bobbing in the grey chop a few hundred yards offshore. These are available at tourist gift shops throughout Cornwall, and so a great many of the fishermen use

'The ruins of the factory were long overgrown, being quietly reclaimed by the land to become shadows on a map'

them as markers for their kit, creating a surreal scene of hundreds of brightly coloured footballs bobbing over some of the more heavily fished areas, as though some bizarre maritime disaster had befallen a ship on its way to Brazil.

'Right, Mont,' said Nige, 'off to Carrick Luz. The net's been down there for a couple of days, and there should be a few crabs in it by now.'

I gunned *Razorbill*'s engine, the clatter of the pistons rising to what was almost a throaty roar – or perhaps more of an arthritic rattle. She turned her nose into the waves, rocking and slamming as we headed towards Carrick Luz, a distinct dark ridge that tumbled from the cliff top into the heaving waters of the bay. This was one of Nige's best sites, a huge reef that extended underneath the surface to a point 200 yards from shore.

'Bit of a blow now, Mont,' said Nige, with unmistakable relish. 'The old girl likes a bit of wind, you know. She's a good sea boat, actually – hopefully you'll get to see her in a big swell before you leave.'

He shrugged into an oilskin top and looked rather proud as the boat muscled her way through the gathering gloom.

Soon we arrived at two blue footballs in the lee of the ridge and Nige quickly hooked them on board, wrapping the line that dangled from them around the winch. He flicked the lever at the bow, the winch whirred into life and the net slowly began to come aboard.

'Right, sit there,' he said, pointing at the cover of the engine box. 'All you need to do is untangle the crabs as they come overboard. There's no simple way of doing it, just get stuck in. It'll take a couple of hours to do the whole net, so settle yourself down and soon we'll have a crab for you to play with.'

Sure enough, after a few moments a shape appeared in the water, angular and mysterious as it was lifted towards the boat.

'She turned her nose into the waves, rocking and slamming as we headed towards Carrick Luz'

And then, clicking and tapping on the wooden decking like a giant insect, our first spider crab was welcomed aboard. It was well and truly tangled in the net, doomed by the same spikes and hard shell that had offered it protection throughout its life. I lifted it into my lap and began the process of untangling it.

Untangling spider crabs from nets – an activity that would feature very strongly in my life for the next month or so – is akin to being handed a Rubik's cube every minute. It's an intellectual exercise with a time limit, carried out on a rocking platform. Each crab was tangled in a unique manner, some entirely swaddled in layer after layer of net, and some – the singularly unlucky ones – with a single bar of the net hooked over one spine. Each had to be handled gently, as you don't want to damage them, and yet no sooner had I carefully disentangled one – my tongue protruding and brow furrowed in concentration – than Nige would hand me another. He chuckled when I glanced up in frustration.

'There's always one more, Mont, always one more.'

The key part of the strategy of netting is that it relies on the fact that the crabs move into the shallows to breed. As such, when a female becomes entangled, several males will follow, lured into the mesh by the oldest and most compelling bait of all – sex. I felt a pang of pity as crab after bewildered crab landed in my lap, writhing and twisting in the deadly cocoon of the mesh. So near to achieving their aim, and yet the urge that saw them close in on a female to create life was the very drive that sealed their fate.

It was while we sat companionably side by side, two men in a small boat rocking off the Lizard, that we began to talk.

'So, Mont, how are you enjoying the fishing so far?' Nige asked casually, both of us entirely absorbed with untangling crabs. 'I'm interested to know what it's been like for you as an outsider.'

I told him of my hopes and fears as I tried to learn the job, of my aching back and weary limbs, and all the while *Razorbill* heaved and pitched in the chop, and the occasional gull settled on the bow to peer at us with a bright, opportunistic eye, feathers ruffled in the stiffening breeze. Slowly the piles of crabs grew in the tubs at our feet and slowly we inched our way along the net.

We talked of how the cottages abutting the shoreline in the cove were now almost exclusively owned by people who had moved in over the last generation. Although Cadgwith had resolutely retained its identity as a fishing community, there was now a healthy mix of outsiders that lived in the village. The fishermen tended to live out of the cove, where houses were more reasonably priced, and make the short commute down the precipitous hill to their boats each morning.

Even the beach was strewn with the evidence of this influx. Dotted alongside the larger hulls of the fishing vessels were numerous punts, dories and sleek fibre-glass hulls used by recreational anglers and occasional visitors – something unimaginable only a century before.

'How do you feel about these other people coming into Cadgwith, Nige?' I asked. 'You're a Cornish boy through and through – is there a bit of resentment there as you've had to move to the Lizard, and hardly any of the fishermen actually live in the village any more?'

Nige paused in his work for a moment to consider this question.

'Well, Mont,' he said finally, 'I actually quite like the English. I think sometimes it can get a bit claustrophobic when it's just us Cornish all living on top of each other in a tiny village, and the outsiders certainly bring something to our community.'

He paused again, looking up at the distant headland that hid the village.

'Nope,' he said, more resolutely this time, 'it's not a problem, it's just modern life, isn't it? They're all right, the English, and I like having them here.'

I opened my mouth to point out that technically Cornwall was in England anyway, then wisely shut it again.

And so we talked for hour after hour. Nige would tell me tales of fishing and the sea, of the old days in Cadgwith and of his hopes for the future of the fleet. He talked of the days when the men of the village would muster as the sun rose, dark figures in the damp half-light, and work as one to heave and shove the boats down the shingle. He talked of the songs that used to echo around the cove and how they turned to a lament when men were lost. He talked of the great hauls and of mysterious, exotic visitors to our shores that occasionally ended up in the nets. He had a well-developed sense of the absurd and relished the genuine comic moments of fishing, the dark humour that seems to emerge in every harsh environment.

'You know, Mont, someone ended up wearing a monkfish as a hat once.' The monkfish is a big animal, sometimes known as an angler fish, with a mouth like

'I felt a pang of pity as crab after bewildered crab landed in my lap, writhing and twisting in the deadly cocoon of the mesh' a wheelie-bin lid lined with viciously sharp teeth. 'It was a big old beast and came up over the winch just as the fisherman glanced behind him. It flipped as it came in, and basically its mouth went straight over his head. It took his mates an hour to get it off, partly because the teeth all face inwards, but mainly because no one could help as they were all helpless with laughter. I mean, it's not a good look that, staggering around the deck with an annoyed 20-pound fish worrying your head, is it?' My laughter echoed against the walls of the great reef that rose out of the sea nearby, as the tide ebbed and swirled around us.

Several hours later the two footballs that marked the end of our day's work bobbed in the water ahead of us.

'Well done, Mont,' said Nige, as he dragged them aboard. 'That's not a bad day's haul when you think about it. Right, the weather's getting a bit poor, so I'd say we need to head home, wouldn't you?'

'Poor' is the fisherman's term for anything from a Force Four that makes working difficult, right the way through to a typhoon that will blow your eyebrows off. As the sea was now flecked with foam being whipped off the crests of angular swells, making *Razorbill* buck and heave beneath me like a colt with the wind in its tail, I did feel that it was indeed a tad 'poor'.

We barrelled our way back to the beach, surfing down the larger swells and battering through the short chop that gathered around the headlands. *Razorbill* gleefully slid onto the beach, the crackling foam at her stern chasing her home. I leapt into the shallows, attached the winch hook and slowly we were pulled up above the tide, with Nige riding aboard like some sedate old carnival queen.

'Right, Mont,' he said, heaving the net box across the deck towards the side of the boat, 'go and get me one of those empty boxes from by the shed and we'll start sorting the net.'

And so began the next phase of the day, when the air was rich with debate and banter. As we slowly pulled the net from one box to another, all the while disentangling seaweed and stones so it could be ready for the next deployment, we were joined by the other fishermen on the beach trudging down the shingle to lend a hand.

As was the Cadgwith way, they sat and chatted as we worked, occasionally leaning forward to pull a particularly large frond of weed from the mesh, or murmuring advice as I got tangled and frustrated with what I was doing. As the net unravelled, 400 metres of nylon passing slowly through our hands, so the conversation flowed and fluxed, sometimes billowing, sometimes snagging, but never quite still.

In that 400 metres we discussed: the state of the net (rubbish, according to Danny), whether we were scared of or attracted to Serena and Venus Williams (Philip and several others), whether outsiders were good in a traditional fishing community (Nige), whether there would ever be a shark attack in Britain (me), whether the Common Fisheries Policy would ever work (everyone) and whether Kate Humble was good-looking (everyone again, as well as a few passers-by dragged in as the casting vote).

And so the conversation echoed around the walls of the cove, its well-head a group of Cadgwith fishermen gathered around a boat and a net. The end of the day was punctuated with a shout of laughter at a ribald comment from Philip, the noise drifting out to sea to be lost in the soft winds of the voices that had gone before.

CHAPTER 4

BEYOND THE LIZARD

Although every skipper on the beach had a distinct character, for me there was one man who stood slightly apart from the rest.

This was certainly not because he was anti-social – quite the opposite in fact – but whereas the rest of the boats tended to fish almost exclusively for crab and lobster, Danny Phillips was a netting man through and through. So I was particularly excited when he offered me a place on his boat for a day.

Danny was a quiet, measured figure with a genuine air of authority about him. He owned *Scorpio*, a sky-blue boat that even to my untrained eye gave the impression of order and compact efficiency. Danny had been the skipper of a trawler in Newlyn and was a constant source of information on legislation and the broader issues affecting the Cadgwith fleet. He was also the proud owner of 'the Loft' – an old shed on the beach that housed all manner of fishing gear and tattered kit, but was also well known as a spot where the hard-core party animals of the cove would retire when the pubs were shut. The atmosphere in the Loft was akin to that of a bunker created by combat-addled veterans in the Mekong Delta in 1971. There was a certain amount of hard drinking, a great deal of air-guitar playing and enough salty anecdotes to make you feel mildly seasick.

Danny was a great thinker about his fishing, highly attuned to the moods of the sea and the movements of his prey. A fisherman by instinct and heritage, he became particularly emotional about some of the more ludicrous legislation facing the small-boat fleet.

As I crunched past on the shingle one morning, carrying a bucket of festering bait towards *Razorbill*, Danny waved me over and gestured for me to climb aboard his boat where he was sifting through piles of nets preparing for the next day's fishing.

'Hello, Mont,' he said, as I clambered over the side. 'I thought you might like to see the latest little dilemma we fishermen find ourselves in. Have a look at this.'

He held up a net, so light it twitched in the breeze and so fine it shimmered like gossamer.

'This net is for catching red mullet and can only be up to 70mm for each mesh. Here we go, have a look.' He held the net between the finger and thumb of each hand, stretching the mesh as he did so. 'As you can see, each mesh – known as the holes in the net to non-fishermen like yourself – only stretches to 70mm. These are the rules, and I went out and bought this net new last season so I would be within those rules. So we're legal. Or at least we were until they introduced the Omega Gauge.'

The concept of net-mesh size is as old as the hills. In 1291 Philip IV of France decreed that the size of the holes in a net should be no smaller than a *gros tournois d'ar*, a common coin of the day. The idea was and is to keep the mesh as large as is reasonably possible so that juvenile fish can slip through the gaps and go on to live happy, fulfilling fishy lives until they are big enough to be caught. In this way the populations of the target fish are maintained at a sustainable level. Ideally the net size for a particular species should allow the fish to grow to a point where it can breed at least once, thus ensuring the survival of one more generation. That's the principle, anyway.

A snag not anticipated by Philip IV (nor, it seems, anyone else since) is that if you use enough force you can push a coin through a pretty small mesh. Your 13th-century French fisherman might have had his net measured by a consumptive peasant with trembling hand who could barely pick the coin up in the first place – meaning that he had to use a bigger net for the rest of the year (and therefore catch fewer fish); or, if he was lucky, by a powerful knight who could force the coin through the tiniest mesh (and possibly the table top beneath), leaving the fisherman with nets like muslin that caught absolutely everything and guaranteed *une saison magnifique*.

Fast-forward 700 years or so and we discover that no one has learnt their lesson. We also discover a rather annoyed Danny.

The snag facing him, and every other small-boat fisherman, is the much-heralded arrival of something called an Omega Gauge. Today, net-mesh size has been refined to the point where you must have certain sizes of mesh for certain species. If you go out to catch cod in a red mullet net, you could end up being prosecuted. Again, all of this is very commendable in theory.

The fishermen dutifully went out and purchased the right nets for what they hoped to catch in the coming season. With the old manually operated gauge – essentially a wedge pushed into the mesh – this worked perfectly well.

But then in the spring of 2005 – after four years of research, three years of development and a joint EU/ICES/ SGMESH/NAFO/FAO (WGFTB) project that spanned scientific disciplines, harnessed international expertise and cost hundreds of thousands of pounds – the gauge by which all other gauges must be gauged was adopted as standard. There was only one problem. It didn't work.

Such was the complexity of the new Omega Gauge, with its wireless technology and multiple settings, that even the fisheries inspectors struggled to use it correctly. This led to threats of legal action from the National Federation of Fishermen's Organisations (NFFO) and demands from MPs representing constituencies with large numbers of fishermen that the gauge be withdrawn altogether. An independent investigation commissioned by the fishing industry noted that although the gauge did measure mesh size – as one would rather hope it would, quite frankly – there were several modifications required to the way it was used on a fishing boat. If it was troublesome for the larger vessels, for the smaller boats it was a complete nightmare.

'The big problem with the Omega Gauge,' said Danny, as he twisted the net between calloused fingers, 'is that it's really set for heavy trawling gear. Mind you, even the trawler boys have had all sorts of snags with it. But when it measures a fine mesh like this, it just stretches it. So suddenly, just because the gauge has changed, all of my nets have become illegal.'

'But surely you must get compensated for the gear you can no longer use,' I asked, although I already had an inkling what his response might be.

'Nope, all the nets I've bought have suddenly become illegal, and there's nothing I can do except buy new ones if I want to catch red mullet.'

He looked at the net in the bin before him, still shining and neatly folded, representing hundreds of pounds of investment.

'But the real problem I have with all this isn't the money, actually. It's the fact that I now have to use a smaller mesh size because the Omega Gauge stretches it so much. And that means, of course, that I catch more small, juvenile fish. Which are undersize and illegal anyway.'

He puffed out his cheeks and once again picked at the net as it fluttered in his hands.

'I don't know, Monty. All of this is supposed to be for the conservation of fish, but I'm struggling with a dilemma here. Either I catch a lot more smaller fish, which can't be good for the stock, or I become a criminal and use the net they told me was fine last year. All because of a bloody gauge.'

I didn't know quite what to say, so instead of keeping quiet I did what I always tend to do in these situations, and said something stupid and pointless.

'A nasty case of gauge-rage, I suppose.'

He looked up and snorted with laughter. 'You have to smile, Monty, otherwise you'd go crazy. Anyway, must get on with this – just thought you'd like to know the type of thing we're up against.'

* * *

Fishing with Danny would mean heading out beyond the Lizard and into the waters leading up to the horizon and the six-mile limit. This was a good idea for a number of reasons.

The first was financial.

When I arrived in Cadgwith I had decided that during my time there, and in my brief career as an embryonic fisherman, I needed a firm aim. Somehow I wanted to judge my progress, to get a measure of how I was shaping up. I was keenly aware that I was only going to touch on the realities – this was, after all, an experiment for me: I was not going to have to rely on fishing for

a living or a career, and after a short period I would return to my life as an errant writer, broadcaster and diver. With that in mind, I had also decided that the money I earned would be donated to the fund used to maintain the winch – although again I didn't anticipate that this would mean a new shed, a gold hawser or installing a nuclear-powered engine. I had an inkling my earnings would be modest, but even so I needed a target.

The annual average wage in Cornwall is about £21,000 – well below the national level. We may have an enduring image of Cornwall as an idyllic haven, all golden beaches and quaint villages, but it has always been a tough place to make a living and faces economic and social hardships even today. Fishing every day of the year is obviously a non-starter and any fisherman has to put money aside for the upkeep of his boat and general costs such as fuel.

I figured that if I could make close to the Cornish average wage for my time as a working fisherman, then I'd be doing well. I had thrown myself wholeheartedly into the three weeks I had put aside for the apprenticeship and not let the finances loom too large. I'd figured – quite perceptively as it turned out – that I would be so utterly incompetent for this early phase that to ask for money as crew would be an insult. It was when I graduated to taking the boat out on my own, to setting my own pots, to crewing on larger boats as a valid member of the team, that I would set my sights on earning money.

Given the average salary and the constraints of not being able to be at sea every day, it seemed to me that earning £100 a day for those periods when I was actually fishing would be a good effort. Whether that would be from directly selling my own produce or from being paid as a crewman remained to be seen, but it seemed as good a target as any.

By the time Danny invited me onto his boat, I was falling slightly short of that target. About £90 a day short, to be precise. A day's crewing should help me claw my way back into something approaching financial respectability, particularly on Danny's boat which had a fine reputation for catching targeted species in considerable quantities.

The second reason I was eager to go out with Danny was that I felt I would learn a great deal from him. He had a reputation as a fastidious and highly professional operator. Watching him at work could only benefit my own rather feeble attempts to catch more fish.

The final reason was that Danny was after monkfish and if there was one species I really wanted to see up close and personal, it was the monkfish.

Here is an animal that only a mother could love. It is ugly in the extreme, and I speak as a man who tries to find the merit in all marine creatures. It is a bruiser, a grinning troglodyte with an undershot jaw and a lumpen body. It looks as though someone has stuck the tail end of a pollack onto a burst sofa cushion using snot as an adhesive. If a monkfish was created in a special-effects studio, the director would tell the advisor to go away and tone it down a bit, and then secretly have him fired. It's a great big children's nightmare of a fish.

We know it better as the angler fish and if there is one beautiful thing about it, it's the fact that it is very good indeed at what it does. This involves lying still on the sea floor, trying hard to look like a rock and twitching the modified tip of its dorsal fin around above its cavern of a mouth. Should a small fish be attracted to what looks precisely like a flickering foodstuff – and a

great many are – that great jaw opens like a trap door. Water is sucked in as a vacuum is created (incidentally, this technique is used by a great many bony fish to feed) and the wicked teeth hold the prey in place. The teeth are a wonder to behold, rank after rank of needle-sharp fangs. They actually fold inwards, allowing a wriggling fish to pass into the mouth, then snapping up like a switchblade behind.

'If there was one species I really wanted to see up close and personal, it was the monkfish'

These ogres of the sea floor can grow to a massive size, and there are valid accounts of them taking seabirds as well as other fish species. In fact should you be snorkelling and spy a large rock with eyes, I suggest you swim away at some speed, particularly if it happens to wave a little ragged flag at you. Monkfish also lay millions of eggs, which float on the sea's surface in great red rafts. Come the apocalypse, only cockroaches, Charlie Sheen and monkfish will remain.

'Good to see you want to do a bit of real fishing,' Danny remarked with a smile, when I said how much I was looking forward to coming along, 'none of that catching crabs in pots nonsense. I'll see you tomorrow at 6.30.'

I was duly to be found pacing the beach the next morning, as keen as mustard to get out into what were, for me at least, the near-mythical fishing grounds beyond the Lizard. I had been warned off these waters again and again. This was not because the other men were particularly protective of

'It's a great big children's nightmare of a fish'

their own sites, it was more that it's a place where billions of gallons of sea water heave over dark pinnacles at the changing of the tides, and where the swell collides with the wind in a mixing pot of swirling currents and furrowed peaks. Such a place is not the realm of a new skipper in a small boat.

Happily Danny was anything but that, and even the weather forecast showing a brisk Force Five rising to a Force Seven didn't seem to deter him. He turned up with his crewman Perry at the appointed time and both of them set about loading bait onto *Scorpio*. It was immediately apparent that Danny ran a tight ship, with everything neatly stowed and a system that spoke of order and calm.

I couldn't help noticing that Perry was wearing a green sweatshirt, which seemed to be tempting fate a little.

'Ah, it's not green,' said Perry when I pointed this out, 'it's emerald.' So that was that cleared up.

We were pushed off from the beach by one of the other fishermen, and Danny executed a neat turn within the confines of the cove before pointing *Scorpio* straight at the Lizard, crouched in the distance full of menace, glowering at this scrap of a boat bustling towards it from the east. I stood near the bow, one hand on the winch, staring flintily at the horizon and feeling every inch the rugged Cornish fisherman.

It was a very different man indeed who came back round that corner eight hours later. A more reflective, more measured and slightly thinner man, pebble-dashed with a crust of dried muesli and semi-digested bits of toast. But on that breezy morning I was blissfully unaware of what lay ahead and I couldn't wait to get out there and begin hauling the nets, set in a mysterious world 200 feet beneath the prying eyes of man.

We steamed for a good hour and a half, pushing out towards the six-mile limit, an invisible boundary for every fishing boat in Britain. *Scorpio* clattered her way south and west, her high prow shouldering aside the steep swells, her superstructure rocking and swinging at the head of a twisting wake. From the shore she must have looked like a mere dot, a tiny blue comet heading for a heaving horizon.

At this point I felt absolutely fine, sitting on the gutting deck at the back of the wheelhouse chatting to Perry, the most amiable and easy-going of companions. There was a certain amount of pitching and heaving going on, but nothing I couldn't handle. I had always sneakily regarded seasickness as something of a flaw, a weakness suffered by those enfeebled by a lack of manly resolve. It was certainly not something to which a swarthy fisherman such as myself would be vulnerable, and I was keen to get on with the business of the day.

Suddenly Danny stuck his head out of the wheelhouse door.

'We're here, fellas. There's the buoy dead ahead. Let's get cracking, Perry.'

Perry leapt to his feet and carefully made his way forward, balancing all the while against the pitching of the boat, which had increased now we had slowed. He hooked the buoy with a large gaffe and quickly tied the line into the winch, flicking it into life with one hand to begin the lifting of the net.

There was over 200 feet of water beneath our keel, so lifting the net took some time. These nets lie on the sea floor like a curtain rising only three feet high, designed specifically to entangle monkfish as they go about their gloomy business. The first net began to move through the winch, and shortly after that I saw Danny peering into the water as a large white shape appeared from the darkness. He turned to me with a wide smile.

'Here we go, Monty, this is what today is all about. Proper fishing, you see – strange shapes appearing out of deep water.'

He kept one hand on the winch, expertly touching the lever to lift the monkfish out of the water so he could swing it on board. It hit the deck with a slithery thump, to lie gasping and gaping as the boat tilted and pitched beneath it. It was the most extraordinary-looking creature, with that strange, frilled, vestigial body dominated by the wicked curve of the mouth. It was essentially a jaw-propulsion system, a hinged portal to oblivion for any small fish that happened to stray within range. It's a wonder that fish of a certain size at a certain depth around the coast of UK aren't permanently on the brink of a nervous breakdown.

The monkfish was once known as the 'poor man's lobster', due to the white meat in the tail. Such was the squeamish attitude to the origins of that meat that it took many, many years for attitudes to change. But now quite the reverse is true. Today monkfish is regarded as a real delicacy, with a price that – ironically – matches or even exceeds lobster.

My thoughts were interrupted by Danny.

'Now that,' he exclaimed, 'is what I'd call a massive cock.'

I should point out at this juncture that male crabs are referred to as 'cocks' and females as 'hens'. This perfectly innocent quirk in nomenclature means that the average fishing trip can very swiftly begin to sound like a bad Benny Hill sketch. This is particularly apt when you consider that the worst type of male crab is one that has just moulted and has not yet hardened – leading to numerous tittering conversations about how disastrous a soft cock is. I was pretty alarmed the first time that subject came up when I was alone on a small boat in the middle of nowhere with just one other chap for company, let me tell you.

Happily Danny was referring to the male crab that was struggling in the netting as it was lifted over the winch. It was indeed an immense specimen, with a massive broad shell akin to a substantial game pie, and great dark pincers held aloft in a last futile gesture of defiance.

'Here we go, Monty,' said Danny, 'could you untangle that for me?'

He handed me the crab, still struggling in the net, and turned back to the winch.

I sat on the gunwale and did as he asked, all the while wary of the claws and entirely focused on the job in hand. This meant concentrating hard, with my head down as the world pitched and corkscrewed around me.

Halfway through untangling the crab, I began to feel quite … unusual. Unbidden I started to breathe heavily and a light sheen of sweat sprang up on my forehead. I glanced up and stared at the horizon, feet planted on the deck to give at least a vague semblance of stability. The blood draining from my face met with a wave of nausea rising from my stomach to form a bubbling cauldron at about chest level. This wasn't going to be pretty, but it needed to happen immediately. I dropped the crab with a clatter on the deck and stood up smartly, turning to grip the rail and, with a bellowed 'Heeeaargh', discharged breakfast into the sea a few feet below. Danny glanced up in surprise.

'You all right there, Mont?' he asked.

'Fine, fine, just fine,' I gasped weakly. 'I'm just, you know, going for a little bit of a lie down.' I looked up with wide eyes,

'It was indeed an immense specimen, with a massive broad shell akin to a substantial game pie, and great dark pincers held aloft in a last futile gesture of defiance'

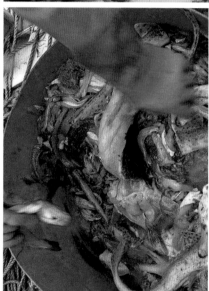

jaw hanging and spittle trailing from my lower lip. Altogether an attractive look, one I couldn't help thinking would only reinforce my credentials as a hard man of the sea.

Mind you, anyone who knows anything about the sea will never, ever be anything other than sympathetic to someone struck down by seasickness, and Danny proved to be no exception.

'There we go,' he said, 'seen it happen to lots of people in my time. Take it easy for a few minutes and see how you get on a bit later.'

I nodded dumbly and wobbled off to the wheelhouse, to slump against the small wooden bench at the rear bulkhead.

And so the morning passed. Every time I stood up to try to join Danny and Perry on deck, a great bank of nausea would descend on me like a rolling storm front, obliterating all logic and reason, and forcing me back into my pitiful foetal position at the stern. I tried various locations around the boat – the snag with fishing vessels being that there really is nowhere to lie down when work is underway – including one remarkable effort when I found myself curled up on a chopping board about 18 inches across.

The problem with this was that Danny was having the haul of his life, with all manner of exciting creatures thrashing their way to the surface. As I lay on the floor of the wheelhouse, I saw giant monkfish, speckled rays, cod, crabs and lobsters frisbee past my feet to the holding boxes at the stern. It was a marine biologist's treasure trove, a sample of life in the deep water beyond the reach of my normal diving excursions, and I was very interested indeed. Sadly my body had turned into a giant organ of evacuation, a big fleshy bellows, and all I could do

was raise one feeble eyebrow at the extraordinary animals passing by the tips of my wellies.

After a few hours even the Lizard Peninsula slipped below the horizon and we were at the limits of the fishing grounds. At this point I was in the midst of perhaps the most enthusiastic bout of chundering of the whole day and had decided after considerable market research that the optimum place to be was the stern, as Danny and Perry were still being highly industrious forward of the cabin and I didn't want to get in their way.

I grabbed the rail with white knuckles between bouts, staring tight-lipped into the middle distance, breathing heavily through my nostrils before leaning forward for the next exuberant hurl. After one particularly enthusiastic effort, I was surprised to find myself in a lovely dark room, which was warm and quiet, and I thought very much about how I didn't want to leave. This thought was rudely interrupted by a searing pain in my left hand, akin to my fingers being slowly squeezed in a vice equipped with tacks meticulously welded in neat rows. It hurt a great deal and made me leave the warm room, which made me sad.

What made me even sadder was that I awoke to find I had passed out and was now rolling in the freezing waters of the scuppers at the back of the boat, gasping and flailing in outrage. I thought it worthwhile to explore the pain in my left hand, which hadn't gone away despite my leaving the warm room. I lolled my head sideways in the ear-deep water and gave my hand a bovine stare. I was alarmed to see that attached to it was a large monkfish, worrying the fingers like a demented terrier. In one of the wilder pitches of the boat, my flaccid form had washed up against a box containing several very annoyed fish. One of my arms had flopped over the side and one of the larger monkfish had clamped on. This is not unreasonable if you think about it, but I wanted it to let go.

'Garagh merb beelbrum...' I mumbled to it out of the corner of my mouth that wasn't submerged, as one rolling fishy eye stared at another. The monkfish just clamped on with yet more vigour, again not an unreasonable course of action in the circumstances. This whole embarrassing situation was resolved by Danny, who arrived round the corner of the wheelhouse to be met by a wide-eyed, desperate stare from the vigorous young apprentice awash at his feet.

'Belurd freh cestrop...' I stated quite clearly, indicating the nature of my predicament with a swivel of my eyes towards the crisis on the end of my arm. Realising that the game was up, the heavily outnumbered monkfish let go, leaving Danny to help me to my feet and guide me into the wheelhouse. I started to explain, but he held up one hand and gestured for me to sit.

'That's it for you, Monty,' he spoke slowly and kindly, rather as one would to a confused pensioner. 'You're to take care of yourself for the rest of the trip. Well done, fella, it's been a good effort. Now, drink some water and don't puke on my fish.'

With that he darted out onto the deck, almost (but not quite) managing to hide a chuckle as he left.

And so the afternoon passed. I lay helplessly in various different bits of the boat, having been ejected from the cabin as Danny had to drive and there wasn't the room for two people, particularly when one of them insisted on lying down and rolling around like a condom full of custard.

When moved from the shelter of the cabin I would crawl through a carpet of slimy fish bits to the bow, to slump amid the net boxes before being moved on again like a tramp who has recently soiled himself.

This went on for five hours.

There was one heroic moment when I rose Lazarus-like from amid a pile of netting and declared myself fully cured. I charged around the deck vigorously, hurling fish boxes around and ferrying crabs to the store pot. I awoke very shortly afterwards, with Danny and Perry leaning over me like oilskin-clad angels. This time it was Perry who spoke first.

'Right, Monty, that's it. You're in the cabin and you're not moving from now on.'

This time I could only mutter something dark and unprintable, and moments later found myself curled up among the oilskins, tools and various bits of electronics that made up *Scorpio*'s wheelhouse floor. Danny would occasionally stick his head round the door, give a brief nod, say, 'Roight on, Mont, roight on', then dart back to his work. I would respond with a twitch of a pale and callow cheek, before lapsing back into my own heinous, nauseous, gloomy, wildly pitching world.

I would venture to say that never, ever, in the long and dramatic history of the Lizard Peninsula, has a man been so pleased to see the lighthouse appear out of the mists. I celebrated by moving a wellie-clad foot slightly and letting the tiniest of hurrahs escape through spittle-covered lips. We were nearly home and I was never going to sea again. I was going to march up the beach, find an internet cafe, go online and buy a house in Birmingham. Or Moscow.

I woke the next morning with a very thick head and a deep sense of disappointment. It was akin to the hangover of my life, without the advantages of the beer drinking, bad

dancing and semi-naked community congas that tended to go before.

Truth be told, I felt that I had let Danny down, and worse still had given a poor account of myself on the boat.

> 'I could not quite shake the feeling that at the first major challenge, the first real test, I had been found wanting'

I had unequivocally failed. Many, many fishermen get sick during the course of their work, but I imagine very few of them swoon like addled spinsters, ending up having to be rescued from the scuppers wearing a monkfish boxing glove. Over the next few days I endured a fair amount of ribbing from the fishermen in the cove; it was all good-natured and yet I could not quite shake the feeling that at the first major challenge, the first real test, I had been found wanting.

* * *

As the fishing continued to improve in what had become a glorious Cornish summer, the cove became a place of frenzied activity. The waters had begun to warm, and beneath the shimmering surface of the sea off the Lizard the brown crabs had massed in the shallows, moving up from deeper water to within range of the pots and the nets. It was the time of seething life, with dolphins moving in pods beneath the cliff walls, their backs glistening in the sunlight, the mist of their breath whisked away on a warm sea breeze. Gannets soared and drifted in blue skies, scanning the water beneath for a flicker of silver, a moment that would see them turn and roll into a steep dive, going from elegant white gliders into darts of predatory intent in the blink of an eye.

And so I began to sense my own transition taking place. Over these few weeks of frantic fishing activity my confidence and knowledge steadily built, meaning that, although I still considered myself an apprentice, I was taking *Razorbill* out on my own far more often. This is not to say that Nige was not a permanent presence on board – it was after all his pride and joy puttering off around the headland on a daily basis in the hands of a ham-fisted skipper. Frequently, as I worked the pots, the radio would hiss into life as Nige checked up on both his boy and his boat.

'Hello, *Razorbill*, hello, *Razorbill*, come in, *Razorbill*, over...'

I would enjoy leaving a delicious pause before answering, knowing that Nige would immediately assume that I had a) crashed into a rock, b) got lost, c) got tangled up in the winch and blown the engine or – more likely – all of the above.

'Hello, Nige,' I would eventually answer, 'this is *Razorbill* – all going well out here, thanks.'

'Ah, *Razorbill*, that's good to hear.'

There would then follow a tissue-thin excuse to justify getting in touch in the first place. 'Just to let you know that it's high tide in an hour.'

'Thanks for that, Nige, I'll bear it in mind.'

'All right, Monts, see you when you get back in, out.'

That would be it for at least 10 minutes, sometimes 20. Then the radio would crackle once again: 'Hello, *Razorbill*, hello, *Razorbill*...'

And so the cycle would continue until I returned, with Nige having worn a deep groove in the shingle of the shore as he paced back and forth like an expectant first-time dad in a maternity ward.

I would love to say that this was a mere distraction from the day's fishing, but actually it was deeply reassuring. As the elder statesman on the beach, Nige always watched over the fleet, carefully monitoring the radio and making sure the men were all in at the end of the day.

* * *

That target of making £100 a day that I had set myself before arriving in the cove – which now seemed an absolute age ago, another time in another world – was based on the assumption that a lobster or crab cost a great deal of money in a restaurant; therefore all that was required was to figure out how to catch a few, and then the cash would roll in. Surely it was simply a case of buying a few pots, spending a few bob on diesel and putting in a bit of hard graft?

During my apprenticeship, I had decided that once Nigel was happy with me taking the boat out on my own, I would set out to fish as intensively as I could for two weeks. This was based on nothing more than a vague notion that this was a good length of time to go really flat out, maximising what I hoped would be my new-found knowledge.

There finally came a momentous day on the beach when Nige turned to me and declared I was ready to take *Razorbill* out entirely unsupervised.

'You will take care, though, won't you?' he said, looking thoughtful. 'It's not you I'm worried about, it's her. I know she's just a bit of fibreglass and timber, but she's a dear old thing who's kept me safe. I suppose you do get attached in a way.'

'I will, Nige,' I said, my heart racing at the prospect. 'If I bend her I've bought her, how about that?' I slapped her plump rump as I walked past, as if to confirm our new relationship.

And so for the next fortnight I headed out of the cove in the morning, sometimes by myself, sometimes crewing for the other fishermen and working the tangle nets as well as the pots. Nige, being the perceptive and canny gentleman he was, could see that I was trying hard to make a go of it alone and stood back from the operation. He occupied himself by painting pictures and weaving a great many withy pots, happily making the most of the annual influx of tourists to the cove. He would occasionally drop in a pearl of wisdom as I sat in the shed sipping a coffee, tired and baffled at the end of another bad day, but in the main he simply moved quietly into the shadows and observed.

On one or two occasions, when it all got too frustrating for him, he would turn up of a morning as I readied the boat and announce that he was coming along as he 'fancied a bit of a trip out today'. In reality this was an opportunity for him to steer the entire operation back on track, providing a touch on the tiller both literally and figuratively. Whether it was moving the pots I had put out or setting a net to dramatically increase my haul of spider crabs, these trips always made a huge difference to my catch for that day.

In the same way that Nige had allowed me to take over *Razorbill* at sea, so he permitted me to take on his contacts for distributing my catch. This was no small gesture on his part, as these distribution channels are the lifeblood of any small-scale fisherman and it can take many years to foster a relationship with a pub, restaurant or marketplace. And so I would stagger up to the Cadgwith Cove Inn at the end of the day to hammer on the back door, presenting the landlord with a bucket of shining lobsters fresh from the sea. I would also wait nervously in the queue of fishermen loading their catch onto the

white lorry from Harvey's, the main distributor of crab and lobster from the cove. As with all things with the fleet, the fishermen would help one another loading great tubs full of brown crab onto the scales at the back of the lorry, each tub weighing 50 or 60 kilograms. And then my turn would come. Amid much good-natured abuse I would lift a pitifully small bucket of crabs from *Razorbill* and walk towards the lorry, hanging my head in shame.

'Mind your back there, Monts,' said Worm one day, 'you need to be careful of damaging the spine lifting massive weights like that.'

Worm was a crab fanatic, loving above all other things the sight of a large brown crab in good condition. He was one of the keenest fishermen in the cove, virtually exploding with frustration when the bad weather set in.

'What do you actually do out there all day?' added Tonks, hair springing from under his baseball cap, as he peered at my catch with genuine bewilderment.

'Aha,' I said, 'the thing is, Tonks, it's not about quantity with Monty Halls Ltd, it's more about quality.'

'Well,' said Philip, turning a scabby, anaemic crustacean in one massive hand, 'I hate to say it, boy, but there's one or two flaws in that statement. One of them being that it's complete bollocks.'

Philip was a giant, a huge barrel-chested figure with a voice that emerged in a great basso rumble. He had been the coxswain of the Lizard lifeboat for many years and knew a thing or two about the hazards and hidden depths of the waters around the peninsula. Nowadays he only fished part-time and spent the rest of his life being very, very funny indeed. He had a splendidly ribald sense of humour and invariably, if there was an explosion of laughter from within the cove, at its source would be Philip.

He replaced the crab in the bucket and glanced up at me.

'Not to worry, boy,' he said, his voice at such a low frequency it could be heard properly only by humpback whales and elephants, 'you keep going. It's very entertaining watching what you bring in your catch – keeps morale up on the beach.'

And so the days rolled on and my fishing efforts continued. I tried, I really tried, but always there was the nagging suspicion that I was not quite up to the mark and that hours and hours of flawed effort were no substitute for the targeted knowledge and precision approach of the men around me. But I had no other option. All I could do was keep heading out of the cove of a morning and hauling my empty pots.

After the two weeks were up, I stumbled into the Old Cellars cafe having just beached *Razorbill* at the end of the day. Still wearing my oilskins, I was red-eyed and crusted with marine detritus. The cafe retains many of the features of the golden age of the Cadgwith fleet, with an old stone arch that looks out onto the beach. As I spread out a ragged pile of receipts I could look straight out at the boats and the sea beyond. The pile of tattered paper before me represented the sum total of my fishing efforts, the cold hard cash that had been handed over in return for my crabs and lobsters, as well as my few days' crewing on other boats.

The cafe was run by Worm's wife Gill and she soon came out to present me with a cup of tea. She always took the time to ask how my fishing was going and made a bit of a fuss of me as I sat and stared into space at the end of the day. A great many people seem to feel they know all about the demands of fishing, but it strikes me that the only ones who can comment with real authority are the men themselves. Hot on their wellie-clad heels, though, are their wives. One supports the other and both are equally important to the entire operation. This is the way it has always been and epitomises the strong bonds that bind any fishing community.

'How many crabs did you catch today?' she asked politely, placing a warm scone in front of me, the rest of the plate entirely covered with a teetering mound of clotted cream and strawberry jam.

'Oh, you know, Gill, one or two,' I said vaguely. She smiled encouragingly and bustled back to attend to the tourists.

Before starting to add up the receipts, I took a moment to consider the economic reality of life as a small-scale fisherman. There is a real danger of jumping to conclusions about the amount of money that can be made – the assumption is that a considerable portion of the £10 or £15 you pay for a crab supper in a restaurant or pub is passed directly onto the fisherman. This would seem logical as the majority of the logistics and all of the danger of acquiring that crab are taken on by the fishermen themselves. Sadly, the economic reality is fundamentally different.

Crab and lobster prices have remained fairly static in the last four years or so due to the presence of larger vessels flooding the market with vast numbers of them. Diesel prices, on the other hand, have risen precipitously. The cost of fuel affects every aspect of a fisherman's life. Obviously there is the diesel to run the boat. Then there are the plastics – petroleum based – to build the pots, and the transport costs of getting them from the manufacturer to the fisherman.

The price of insurance increases commensurate with the value of the fishing gear, and of course there are the costs of the boat and the licence to run it (these two figures are pretty much equal, incidentally). Most fishermen in the UK have to source a bank loan to purchase these two items, so there is the additional burden of funding the interest and repayments.

An initial assessment of my receipts produced a refreshingly large figure – £695, in fact. This was added up, rather appropriately, on the back of a grubby envelope with an old pen. Although this was nothing like the sum I had originally hoped for – in fact it was almost precisely half – it still represented a reasonable return and I allowed myself the briefest moment of feeling vaguely smug.

Then I subtracted the cost of the bait I had used. Then the cost of the fuel. Then the cost of my contribution to the winch fund and the upkeep of the tractor. Then the cost of my insurance. At each stage the large figure became progressively smaller, its decrease running almost directly in proportion to my rising sense of alarm.

After a few wild-eyed, brow-rubbing moments, the figure before me now sat at £508. Another swift calculation revealed that this was approximately £36 a day for the last fortnight – £36 for getting up at dawn, for hauling pots until my back ached, for hurling my breakfast over the gunwales while being savaged by a monkfish, for hour after hour of toil and emotion.

This didn't even take into account any payments I would have had to make for the cost of equipment (I had simply used Nige's). And of course I didn't have too many of the normal costs of life while I stayed in the Old Cellars – the fripperies and luxuries that make our existence enjoyable and comfortable.

I sat back and exhaled extravagantly, lacing my fingers behind my head as I did so. I looked out through the arch and onto the beach. The boats of the fleet sat high on the shingle, their day's work done. Despite everything I had learned, it was still a powerfully evocative scene, the brightly coloured hulls contrasting with the rich hues of a late-afternoon sky. It was a scene that spoke of romance and drama, with the dark sea behind the boats full of mystery and promise.

The contrast between the row of boats on the beach and the row of numbers on the paper before me was stark indeed. To be a small-boat fisherman in Britain today is to defy financial logic, to fly in the face of simple economic sense. More than ever I realised that the men who skipper and who crew, who wake before dawn and retire young with aching joints, don't go to sea for the money. They are fishermen because they don't know how to be anything else. They simply don't know how to turn their backs on the sea. By their presence they honour the memory of their forefathers and prepare the fishing grounds for their sons.

* * *

It was a measure of Danny's tolerance rather than of my standing in the cove that saw him extend another invitation to join him on a trip several weeks later. By then we were in late summer and the crab fishing was particularly good. But Danny, as ever, was after fish, and not just any old fish. One species had begun to be caught and the news of its arrival swept the cove like some sort of fever. There was a palpable sense of anticipation among all the fishermen as net bins were hauled out from the back of dusty lofts, mesh inspected and floats strung together on new lines. Out in the deep water, the red mullet were moving inshore and, as they had done through the ages, the fishermen of Cadgwith prepared for their arrival.

The red mullet is a gorgeous ruby wedge of a fish with dense flesh that commands a premium price. They are caught at dusk using nets set only a few hours previously. It is a form of fishing that harks back to another time, when the shoals were actively hunted as the light bled from the day, as though the sun were being absorbed into the sea and captured in the red flanks of the mullet themselves. Every fisherman had his favourite location, the co-ordinates of which were a closely guarded secret. They were talked of as seams of gold, passed down from father to son, written as scrawled notes in well-thumbed log books.

Jamma Phillips, Danny's son, was plainly a chip off the old block. He and his brother Tommy were keen fishermen in their own right, despite being only 11 and 15 years of age respectively: on many an evening I would see them heading out of the cove in a small punt to set their own nets or haul their pots. One afternoon I bumped into Jamma as he was mending an old net by the Stick – generally the way the youngsters in the cove acquired their kit was by scavenging the discards from other fishermen – and asked him what he was up to.

He looked up, regarding me with profound suspicion. He paused briefly and then glanced down at the net in his hands.

'I'm mending a net,' he said finally.

'Good stuff. Where do you think you'll put it?' I asked politely, having seen their brightly coloured buoys bobbing either side of the entrance of the cove.

This question elicited an even longer pause for thought. Then he visibly

'The red mullet is a gorgeous ruby wedge of a fish with dense flesh that commands a premium price'

brightened and looked me straight in the eye with a defiant tilt of the chin.

'In the sea,' he said, before bending back to his work to indicate that the conversation was over.

I told this story to Danny as we headed out the next afternoon, preparing to hunt for the red mullet later that night. He laughed delightedly.

'Really, did he say that? That's terrible, I'll have a word.' He half-heartedly shook his head and looked very happy indeed, secure in the knowledge that the family secrets lay secure in their vaults.

Later that night we lifted nets under the deck lights, with red mullet embedded like jewels in the shining mesh. Mixed in among them were the predatory silhouettes of pollack, the occasional haddock, the mottled shapes of some hefty cod and one or two brightly spotted wrasse. It felt wonderful, working in a pool of light in the whispering blackness of the sea that surrounded us. The lights of the cove were obscured by the cliff walls, plunging the coast into a profound darkness that made it just another part of the night that surrounded us. We might have been hundreds of miles offshore as opposed to fishing just within striking distance of the cliffs.

After several hours of good fishing, Danny fired up the engines and turned *Scorpio* for home. As we motored parallel to the coast the lights of Cadgwith magically materialised around the headland, a shining haven in the dark fortress of the Lizard. I was looking forward to the crunch of the bow on the shingle and that oft-repeated final weary trudge up the slope to the pub. But as we drew close to the beach Danny stilled *Scorpio*'s engines, causing her to wallow untidily in the low swell. He emerged from the wheelhouse, looking distinctly preoccupied as he made his way past me to the stern.

''Scuse me, Monty, I've now got to do a job that breaks the heart of every fisherman. I've got to throw most of the catch back.'

I looked at him aghast.

'That's right. The rules mean that I'm only allowed 30 per cent weight of other species compared to the weight of the red mullet I've caught. It's supposed to be a conservation measure, but of course the snag is that I never know how many red mullet I've caught until the end of the night's fishing, so I have to keep everything else in case I have a bumper final haul. That means all the other stuff I've kept is dead, of course – pollack, haddock, wrasse, sometimes even monkfish – but most of it has to be chucked back anyway.'

He moved over to the box of red mullet and quickly weighed it.

'We've got 20 kilograms of red mullet there – not a bad haul, if I do say so myself – and that means I can keep six kilograms of other species that we've taken tonight. If you look in that other box, you'll see what else we've caught – there's some really nice, fat, healthy commercial fish in there. I'd say there's about the same in weight actually, about 20 kilos or so. Some bureaucrat, a very long way from here, has decided that I have to chuck most of it over the side of my boat. In fact, you'd better do it – it makes me sick to the stomach.'

He took one last look at the box of fish, fresh from the sea and shining in the glow of the deck lights, and turned on his heel to walk wordlessly back into the wheelhouse.

And so it was left to me to tip the catch back into the sea, watching it twist and spin slowly through the dark water until it disappeared from view, lost to the crabs, the gulls and to yet more mystifying legislation.

CHAPTER 5

DANGEROUS WATERS

Autumn arrived like a grey wraith, creeping in from the horizon with its chill dawns and rolling mists.

The complexion of the Lizard changed in subtle stages, with the vibrant colours of late summer replaced by gentle pastels. The sea retained the memory of long hot days, warm to the touch, and rose up in eerie banks of mist as the land cooled dramatically before it. As I drifted off to sleep after a day's fishing, I would hear the mournful tones of the foghorn on the Lizard, an echo muffled and then lost as it was carried towards a blurred horizon. It was always a deeply comforting sound, a sentinel call from the tip of the peninsula guiding the fleet home, punctuating my dreams as I travelled the tides in my sleep.

To go fishing in these conditions was to occupy a world of dimmed senses, where vision and sound played tricks. Even though on *Razorbill* we were only puttering round the corner from the cove, we would still occasionally lose the cliffs completely in the fog and find ourselves motoring through a new, altogether more sinister world. Here the rustle of the waves against the rocks was reduced to a disembodied murmur, a metallic sound that chuckled and sang as it tried to lead us astray. As we peered into the gloom that enveloped us, it seemed that every shifting bank and rolling cloud took the form of a vast tanker bearing down on our fragile little boat; then abruptly the mist would dissipate, a dark vision borne away on the breeze.

Gone were the gentle dawns of summer, when the cove rang almost every day to the shouts of the men as they readied the boats to go to sea. Now hunched groups gathered in the darkness of the early morning, muffled figures stamping their feet to keep warm as they muttered about the conditions. For the first time the sea began to show a different face, one that was grey and brackish, flecked with dead seaweed that piled on the beach in festering mounds. There seemed to be a new venom in the swell as it licked at the dark walls of the cove, carrying the energy of distant storms in thick peaks that smashed and hissed into the black rocks.

The number of mornings when the fleet was forced to stay ashore increased, with the boats sometimes motionless for three or four days in a row. During these periods the fishermen took on other roles, part of their own transition into the routine of winter, and it was not unusual to see plumbing or roofing equipment being loaded into vans that had once held pots and nets.

Although fog and squall were the signature of the change of seasons, there were occasional moments of stillness that provided some of the most breathtaking days of my time in Cadgwith. These saw crystal-clear dawns, when the chill seemed to make every sound crack and ring in the air and when the sea stilled its restless passage, settling into a sheen of molten bronze as the sun touched the horizon. On these days we would head to the fishing grounds, passing cliffs devoid of tourists and walkers, and we would feel energised by the cold. Our breath would fog and our fingers would tingle, and yet there was the sensation of coming alive. There is nothing quite like a still day in a temperate autumn, holding a hint of the winter to come, and Nige assumed a look of quiet contentment as we went about our work.

'It's probably my favourite time of the year, you know, Mont,' he remarked as we began to haul the pots. 'You feel like another year is passing and every calm day is a bonus. The fishing is pretty good, too, lots of crabs around, which always improves the mood.'

But there was another face to the change of the seasons. With the end of the summer came the potential for menace and mayhem, for swift and violent change. I had very little experience of being in a small boat in a big storm, and as *Razorbill* bucked and twisted in the squalls that seemed to pass through the fishing grounds ever more regularly, I would occasionally glance at Nige for reassurance. He would nod in my direction, before turning his gaze to the horizon. I may have had little experience of the harrowing fury of an Atlantic storm, but Nige had memories that tempered every decision he made.

* * *

It began with just a ripple. A tiny feathering of the surface far out to sea in the immense open spaces of the Atlantic. Warm air, rising from the equator, fell back to earth as it cooled, landing gently on the ocean to dissipate with nothing more than a sigh that drifted across the water beneath. As yet more air fell it began to gyrate in a massive, lazy spiral, driven by the rotation of the earth itself.

The spiral grew in strength and soon became a vast whirlpool of wind, gaining power as more and more errant siroccos were drawn towards it. The surface of the sea, far from the gaze of man, began to thrash and heave in short, choppy peaks, convulsing under the opposing forces driving it back and forth. The earth imperiously rolled beneath what had become a low-pressure system, bringing continents within reach, ferrying them towards roiling swells and gun-metal clouds. Abruptly the storm combined with another, their two edges meeting to intensify their power, different air pressures skidding and sliding in tandem to double and treble the wind speed. The winds rose to hurricane force, their howl became a shriek and the front rolled towards Europe, carrying with it immense oceanic forces that heaved within the great depth of the water beneath them as they charged towards the east.

The dark border of the hurricane was now advancing like a bombardment, churning the sea into a no-man's land of craters and explosive peaks, with swells racing ahead as a reconnaissance force for the chaos that followed. Many miles ahead of the storm, high clouds created a mackerel sky scudding and drifting over the land, the first sign of the immense violence that was as yet below the horizon. A beautiful dusk belied the horror of the night to come, as the last light of the day gilded low clouds a deep red, before the sun finally slipped away. This left only profound darkness, illuminated by the strobing of lightning on the horizon and accompanied by distant echoes that cracked and thumped like far-off artillery.

It was the night of 19 December 1981 and when the force of the spiralling low-pressure system hit the immovable mass of the Cornish coast, it would change many lives for ever. The impact was explosive: all the power previously contained in the deep water of the Atlantic was channelled and focused by the shallow reefs, the waves marshalled like rows of giants that hurled themselves at the dark buttresses of the land in their path. It was a merciless assault. The voices of the waves combined in the roar of battle, a deep growl that was punctuated only by the boom of the cliffs as they repelled attack after attack. Above all was the banshee shriek of 100-mile-an-hour winds, filling the air with spray so that the boundary between water and air became blurred. It was a night when no living thing was out in the open, when the birds and animals on the peninsula trembled in burrows or on ledges, hidden in the darkness and awaiting the dawn.

'Time and again she returned, battered and torn, to come to the aid of those on board'

And yet there was movement. A stricken freighter rolled and pitched in the grip of the storm, powerless as the cliffs drew ever closer, their presence in the night indicated only by the shuddering impact of the waves and the occasional glimpse of white water sluicing and hissing at their base. On board the freighter were eight souls, unwitting bit-part players in what would become one of the greatest dramas in British seafaring history. Hovering overhead was a rescue helicopter, reduced to a helpless and horrified onlooker by both the wind speed and the inability to lift anyone off a vessel that heaved and tossed 60 vertical feet at a time in its death throes.

Against all reason, a much smaller vessel smashed through the waves alongside the freighter. It was an impossible scene, absurd in its ambition, and yet the tiny lifeboat came alongside again and again, driven by the elemental urge to assist and the deep-rooted traditions of the men who crewed her. Time and again she received deadly blows as she was hurled against the metal cliff of the freighter's hull, and time and again she returned, battered and torn,

to come to the aid of those on board. As the helicopter left the scene, low on fuel, the pilot saw the lifeboat lifted by a single giant breaker onto the very deck of the freighter, exposing her stout belly before tumbling back into the sea. And yet again she shook her bright shoulders, gathered her stern, a steady hand pushed forward on the throttles and she hurled herself once more towards the larger vessel.

Several miles along the coast in Cadgwith the red flares glowed against a Valkyrie sky as the men of the Lizard lifeboat were called to duty to assist one of their own. Through the village came hunched figures, leaning into the wind, eyes narrowed against the rain, all converging on the lifeboat shed. The village had prepared well for the storm and the men ran past windows shuttered against the elements, past the fishing fleet pulled into the narrow streets beyond the reach of the waves.

Cadgwith sits cupped by the valley around it, protected by the high cliffs on either side, although even here the residents lay awake listening to the fury of the storm, fearing the worst. These people knew the sea better than most, yet tonight was somehow different. When the men reached the relative sanctuary of the lifeboat shed and began preparing to enter the maelstrom outside, they were pensive and tense. They worked quietly and with grim purpose. The words of one of their forebears hung, unspoken, in the air between them: 'We have to go out. We don't necessarily have to come back.'

And go out they did, into the psychotic fury of that end-of-day storm. The 17 miles to Mount's Bay would normally take them two hours, but on that night it took nearly six. There they searched for a day and a night before being ordered to limp home to the Lizard, subdued and bereft.

Behind them they left the scene of one of the great disasters in the history of the RNLI. Eight men lost, ripping the heart out of the small community of Mousehole from where the Penlee lifeboat hailed. They had launched to go the aid of the stricken freighter, *Union Star*, which had also been lost – all eight people on board swept into the sea within touching distance of the cliffs. There is evidence that at least two of them had already been transferred onto the lifeboat, an act of superhuman seamanship in the teeth of the immense forces the men of Mousehole faced on that dark night.

'I thought of those men lost, of the Christmas presents beneath the tree in their houses and of their empty shoes in their lifeboat shed, and I cried'

As the Lizard lifeboat rounded the headland towards the sanctuary of the shed the next day, the young man at the helm remarked that she was handling rather heavy, sluggish in her response to the tiller.

'You're probably just a bit tired,' said the coxswain. 'We're nearly home now.'

As the boat pulled up the ramp with a rattle of hawsers and chains – journey's end – the exhausted crew glanced down and saw tons of water sluicing out of her shattered bilge keels. Their lifeboat was mortally wounded, broken and battered having fought for over 40 miles through an Atlantic hurricane. A few more big waves, a few more hours and yet more

grim statistics could well have been added to the terrible night that would forever be known as the Penlee disaster.

The young helmsman shrugged out of his equipment and went home. He walked upstairs, ran a bath and climbed in. It was only then, after a night and day of unbearable strain and herculean effort, that he finally cracked.

'I don't mind telling you, Mont,' says Nige, as we sit quietly talking in the shed one afternoon 30 years later, 'and I'll tell any man who asks. I thought of those men lost, of the Christmas presents beneath the tree in their houses and of their empty shoes in their lifeboat shed, and I cried.'

* * *

It was a beautiful calm day early in my apprenticeship, the sort of morning when the whole scheme seemed a rather splendid idea. As we steamed away from the cove prior to commencing the day's fishing, Nigel casually turned to me and said , 'Right, Mont, I think you should jump overboard.'

We were about a mile offshore, the cliffs looming large on the horizon and *Razorbill* creating a gentle, rustling wake that sparkled in the midday sun. The sun was warm on the back of my neck, I was in shirt sleeves, the tiller twitched gently in one hand and all was very much well with the world. I smiled uncertainly.

'Sorry, Nige, for a brief moment there I thought you said I should jump overboard.'

'I did. And what's more I think you should do it right now, right here.'

It is written into Naval Law that if your skipper goes insane you are allowed to take control of the vessel by the use of force. I briefly considered wrestling Nige into one of the larger containers on board and

sitting on it until we got back to Cadgwith. But he looked quite sane, in fact he looked positively serene.

'Look, it's a beautiful day and you're about to take over my boat. Soon you'll be fishing all the way to Black Head on your own and if you fall overboard you need to know what to do. I would have given you more time to prepare, but when I think about it you don't get time to prepare in real life, do you? Now, overboard, please.' He gestured helpfully towards the edge of the boat and the water beyond.

'It's very odd indeed to be dry and entirely in control of your situation one minute, then cold and battling with overly buoyant wellies the next'

'Nige, is this strictly necess...' He raised a weathered hand and gestured again. I had seen Nige heave very large pots into the sea with no more than a flick of a thick wrist, and was fairly confident that a wriggling apprentice could be dispatched with equal aplomb. I sighed miserably, hooked one leg over the gunwale and looked back at him with very large cow eyes. He gestured yet again, this time with slightly more relish, so I swung the other leg over and tipped forward into the sea.

All manner of interesting things happened pretty much straight away.

The first sensation was shock. It's very odd indeed to be dry and entirely in control of your situation one minute, then cold and battling with overly buoyant wellies the

next. The primal creature within railed against this new, rather unpleasant environment and decided that a massive breath was a splendid idea. I gasped and immediately inhaled an unpleasant mixture of foam and spray. Then I started coughing.

Suddenly, with a sharp bang followed by a virulent hiss, my head was seized on either side as I sprouted massive, bright orange breasts that ran all the way up my chest and round the back of my head. This was my life jacket inflating, cupping my face and forcing my features into a puckered gurn of which the only items I could move with any control were my eyes. All I could see was the back of Nige's head as *Razorbill* moved away. He raised one hand behind him by means of farewell and then settled into what was unequivocally a course directly away from his crewman and towards Cadgwith. *Razorbill* began to look very small; by contrast the sea around me began to look very big indeed. I drew my knees to my chest, wrapped my arms around my legs and considered my situation.

The result of falling overboard is a sudden immersion in an icy sea as your boat steams serenely away from you. There is every chance this will happen in the dark, or when the state of the sea is less than ideal – statistically these are the optimum conditions for falling overboard, after all. How must it feel to watch the stern lights fade into dusk or to hear the throb of the engine soften into the wind, and then to face the fact that you are alone?

Unbeknown to me I had already survived one of the more prevalent silent killers. As I hit the water, the blood vessels had constricted in my skin, driving blood flow towards my core and dramatically increasing my heart rate. As a body bobs upright in the water the pressure on the

TO
THE MEMORY OF
TONY CULMER
AND
PETER WILLIAMS
LOST AT SEA 4 MARCH
1994
COME TO ME I LOVE THEE THY
PRECIOUS SOULS I'LL KEEP

RESCUE

FY 781

chest – known as hydrostatic pressure – combines with this sudden increase in the pulse to place a huge strain on the heart. This may well result in a stroke or a cardiac arrest. If there is a weakness in the circulation, the sea will find it. In fact, 10 per cent of drowning cases are found with no water in their lungs, a phenomenon known as dry drowning.

By stark contrast, I was gasping and spluttering in the first few moments of plunging through the surface. I could certainly feel a tightness in my chest, combined with a shallow hitching of my lungs that caused them to twitch and convulse in a series of short ventilations. In 10°C water (about the average temperature of the sea around Britain over the course of a year), the body's instant response is to increase respiration by 600 to 1000 per cent, with each breath taking in about three litres of air. There was no doubt that my body was panicking, desperately trying to ventilate my system for this new and hostile environment.

Even these first few involuntary gasps can be fatal. Fortunately, because I was wearing a life jacket, I was floating high in the water; if I had been lower and had taken in seawater as I inhaled, it would have set off a chain of reactions within my lungs, none of them pleasant. As a salty fluid, the sea water would immediately have initiated a series of fluxes of fluid and plasma into my alveoli – the small sacs where oxygen exchange takes place between the lungs themselves and the capillaries circulating blood around the body.

You might think, therefore, that the smart move would be to hold your breath. This is a perfectly reasonable assumption, but when you are immersed in water at 10°C powerful reflexes kick in that mean the average person can hold their breath for only six seconds. One breath after this – should you happen still to be underwater at the time – means death. In fact, 60 per cent of the drownings around Britain are down to this effect – the cold-water shock causing a reflex breath that takes in water in fatal volumes.

I had now been in the water for over three minutes, and even though I could feel my heartbeat slow and my breathing stabilise as my body slowly came to terms with its predicament, my fingers were becoming numb and my movements clumsy. I pulled my knees up to my chest and held my elbows close to my side, trapping as much heat as possible in a battle with the cold grip of the ocean. It was a battle I knew perfectly well that I would ultimately lose.

Even in tropical waters, hypothermia will set in given enough time. Here in the relatively temperate waters of the North Atlantic there is a no-nonsense approach to sapping the life from any land-based creature that falls in unprotected: survival times are measured in a few desperately uncomfortable hours.

After about 50 minutes of immersion, my body temperature would have dropped by a precious degree to 36°C. After one or two hours, it would be down to 34°C. This is a very, very dangerous place for the body to be, and by now the desperate attempts of the heart and circulatory system to maintain life – driving blood to the core and restricting flow to the extremities – would see the brain deprived of oxygen. This in turn would lead to confusion and nausea. After two to three hours the core temperature would drop still further – to 30°C and below. This is severe hypothermia and will result in death unless the incoherent, trembling, helpless wreck of a casualty is immediately rescued.

So if you unexpectedly fall into the sea

from a boat anywhere around our coast you have a few hours at best, assuming you survive the initial immersion. On earth there are a great many hostile environments for the soft-skinned, naked creature that is man, but the crackling waters of the Atlantic must surely rank among the most unforgiving.

My thoughts on my imminent mortality were – happily – interrupted by Nige performing a tight turn in *Razorbill* and heading towards me flat out, before executing a neat nautical handbrake turn to stop immediately beside me.

'You all right there, Mont?' he asked cheerily. 'Thought I'd get nice and close so you don't have to swim too far.'

I had now been in the water for about 10 minutes, one of the side effects of which was my lips becoming somewhat numb. This in turn meant that I struggled to pronounce my 'f's and my 'sh's, which was probably just as well.

'Good, good,' said Nige, completely ignoring my mumbled expletives, 'now, let's see if you can get back on board, shall we?'

I was very, very keen to get back into *Razorbill* by this stage, so I swirled and waddled my way over to her white gunwales and lifted the two pointless tubes of meat that used to be my arms far enough to hook my lifeless bony fingers over the side.

'Up you come,' said Nige, adding helpfully, 'I won't give you a hand because if it happens for real I won't be here, of course.'

I made it on the third attempt. If I had fallen back into the sea on that last effort, there would have been simply no way I could summon the energy to haul my body up again. Nige looked delighted that I was back on board, as it gave him a chance to fire a series of very enthusiastic questions at me about how I had felt physically and what it had been like to watch *Razorbill*

disappear into the distance – a line of questioning I couldn't help thinking he was basing on many a bitter loss within the fishing community.

As he turned the boat back to the cove and I clambered out of my wet kit and into some spare dry clothes he had thoughtfully brought along, I was still trembling, but already I could feel the sun warming my flesh and the hot ache of blood returning to my fingertips. Without looking at me, Nige began to speak again, this time altogether more quietly.

'You see, Mont, that's the thing with single-handed fishing. You're here alone, and if you go in, there's only you that can get you out. I've lost a lot of friends over the years – good men who have gone over the side or whose boats have foundered. I hope you don't mind, but that's the reason I thought you should understand what you're doing when you go out of the cove on your own.'

He looked ahead once again, lost in his thoughts.

'It only takes a moment, you see, and there's one more fisherman lost. Always wear a life jacket, always remember today and let's make sure you see the year out, eh?'

He finally glanced across at me as the cliffs of the cove slipped by on either side, with that customary half smile that hid a lifetime of knowledge: 'Roight on, Mont, roight on.'

* * *

I was desperate to make a genuine contribution to the fishing effort of the cove, to somehow assist not only Nige but the other fishermen as they went about their business. For these first few weeks, it had seemed that everything I did was slightly wrong and I felt immensely frustrated that I seemed to be more of a hindrance than a help. I was always treated with great patience and tolerance, although this was more a measure of the men of the fleet than of my own ability. It must be quite something to finish an exhausting day's fishing, then when you get ashore have to deal with a bounding simpleton lifting the wrong crates into the wrong lorry, clipping the winch on to the wrong vessels and generally being a large spanner in an otherwise seamless system.

I was therefore absolutely delighted when there was a knock on my door one day and I opened it to find John Trewin standing there. John was the skipper of *Silver Queen* and one of the fittest men I have ever met in my life. All fast-twitch energy and combustible enthusiasm, he stacked and deployed his pots entirely by hand, and as such was as lean as a bullwhip. He was an irrepressible character and seemed to live his life at several hundred miles an hour. He was also Cornish to his bootstraps.

'Morning, Monty,' he would say as the fleet prepared for sea, 'everything under control?' He would then give a shout of laughter and the widest of smiles before trotting off to begin work.

One morning he called me over to the boat, proudly pointing out a painting of a chough on his wheelhouse door.

'See that, Monty, see that? Now, that's a chough, and whenever I go out fishing the first thing I check is that there's a glint in its eye. You can't go wrong when there's a twinkle in the eye of the chough, you know.' He patted it affectionately and sped off (John was a great one for speeding off).

John's crewman was away for a few days so, with a look of faint disbelief that he was even asking the question, he had decided that I might be able to help him out.

'It's just one day, Mont, but it would be a real help. It doesn't have to be today, but if you came along soon we'd try to do

10 strings of pots, you see, and that extra pair of hands would be very useful indeed. What do you say?'

I was thrilled that he had even thought to ask and enthusiastically agreed. I was tied up working with Nigel on *Razorbill* for the next two days, but could certainly help out after that.

> **'And so it began. Five hours of intense work recovering, opening, baiting and stacking pots'**

'Good man, good man,' said John. 'I'll see you the day after tomorrow, then.'

The great day dawned and I hurried down to the beach with that distinct 'first day at school' feeling. John was already scuttling about and welcomed me aboard.

'Nice to see you, Monty. Right, let's get to work – see that bucket of bait? It needs to be cut up. That's your job – I'll get us off the beach and out to the gear.'

I set about the bait with gusto, hacking and sawing away at the festering remains of dogfish and horse mackerel as the boat rumbled to life beneath me. As we motored towards the horizon John would periodically charge out of the wheelhouse to peer over my shoulder, using one grimy finger to point out where I was going wrong (which was pretty much everywhere). After 40 minutes of frantic bait preparation, his voice echoed from the wheelhouse.

'Flag ahoy, Monty! Let's see if you can stack these pots like a Cornishman.'

And so it began. Five hours of intense work recovering, opening, baiting and stacking pots. Each had to be placed carefully on the canting deck, having been carried at waist height to the appropriate location on board. All of this was done at frantic pace – a pot on deck is not catching any crabs, after all, so it was imperative to remove the crabs as quickly as possible and get the pots back in the sea where they belonged. Every string consisted of 30 pots in a line and my job was to bait them and stack them as they came aboard. So I lifted, tottered my way across the deck, stacked the pot neatly and charged back just in time for the arrival of the next. Back and forth, back and forth, all the while carrying, weaving, bobbing and lifting. When all 30 pots were stacked, John gave a triumphant thumbs up, gunned the engine and bellowed at me to begin hurling them back overboard. He was not one for dawdling, so this meant charging forward at full throttle as I frantically heaved the pots over the gunwale, each one connected to the next, each one pulled by a line that was as tight as a steel bar, dragged into the sea by the weight of the other pots and *Silver Queen*'s considerable forward momentum.

No sooner had we deployed one string of pots, then another flag would heave into view and the whole routine would begin once more. With each pot weighing approximately 15 kilograms, and 30 to a string, it meant that by the time we had done seven strings – recovering every single one by hand and then throwing each one back over the side – we had moved 6,300 kilograms between us, a cool six tons. I was drenched in sweat, my lower back was bellowing in protest and, although there might have been a glint in the eye of the chough, mine had assumed the glassy stare of the terminally knackered.

This presented me with a new and not altogether pleasant sensation. We all have a defining characteristic, something on which we hang our hat, and mine has always been very much my physicality. During my time in the Marines, I would say with some confidence that I never had the highest echelons of command looking nervously over their shoulders, not being what you might term a hard-charging career prodigy. On one occasion, after considerable thought, my commanding officer described me in my annual report as 'quite tall' – which is undeniably true, but hardly a recommendation for the giddy heights of command. But although I may have been less than a shining light tactically, by God I could run all day. If there was a man in the Marines they wanted to drop behind enemy lines to do sit-ups at a secret location, I would have been selected immediately. Physically I had relished every challenge presented to me, something I had carried with me into my civilian life. My body had never, ever let me down, carrying me up precipitous hills and grinding out prodigious hours.

Yet here, for the first time, was work that seemed to be getting the better of me. Try as I might, I simply couldn't stack the pots quickly enough. I couldn't wrestle them into position. I couldn't get the bait in before the next one arrived on deck and I could just about hurl them all overboard if I worked absolutely flat out. The boat's engine might have been hammering and roaring as we deployed the pots, but my personal pistons were also going like the clappers, with several warning lights coming on and one or two klaxons sounding for good measure.

'Come on, Mont,' John would shout as I fumbled yet another pot, 'I'm doing your job for you here.' He would scuttle past, fixing one of my more wobbly stacks before returning to the winch.

'You've got to use the roll of the boat,' he

said after the fourth (or possibly fifth, or maybe the sixth) string had gone back overboard. 'At the moment you're fighting the sea, and it's a battle you'll never win. As the boat deck goes in one direction, you need to go with it, then as it comes back you need to pause. It's actually quite simple.'

I glanced up at him as he spoke, the sweat shining on my face, my jaw wide as I heaved in great gasps of sea air, my arms aching and fingers raw. I was about to say something pithy, when he turned once more to the horizon.

'Here we go, another flag! Excellent, I imagine you're fairly warmed up by now.'

And so it all began again, this test of artisanal fitness that bordered on lunacy. The really annoying thing about all this was that John – and indeed the rest of the fishermen – had absolutely no idea how fit they were. They had a positively Dickensian work ethic, a brutal, uncompromising approach to getting the job done that was forged in days past and had never changed. In my own way I was quite proud of how I managed to keep going on *Silver Queen*, stacking and deploying pots for hour after hour, and yet John seemed to regard me as – and I struggle to find the right expression here – a bit of a jumped-up media ponce.

We finally finished the seventh string and were once again surging for another flag when the pitch of the engine changed, a distinct rise in tone that was a fair reflection of my own physiology at that point. A puff of white smoke appeared from the stern, dissipating over the wake to twist and spin on the wind.

John cursed and ran out of the wheelhouse to hang over the back of the boat, peering intently at the outflow of the engine.

'Ah, bugger it,' he said, 'that'll be a bit of seaweed in the water intake. It happens this time of year – after a big tide and a bit of a blow you get loads of weed floating in the water. We could carry on, but it might damage the engine and by the sound of things she's well bunged up. Would you mind if we headed back in? I'll clear it out on the beach. Sorry, Monty, we had three more strings to do as well.' He looked genuinely sad, as though somehow he had let the side down.

I held up a philosophical hand.

'No, John, really, what's most important is the safety of the boat and your engine. I mean, obviously, I'm disappointed and all that, but if we need to head back then so be it.'

John smiled and went back into the wheelhouse, allowing me a brief opportunity to dance a small jig of delight on weary legs as his back was turned. The Judas Jive, you might term it, or the Brutus Ballet. I felt bad for John, I really did, but I was dealing with two powerful sensations. The first was that I was knackered. The second was that we were going home early.

As we headed slowly back to the cove, I reflected on the day. There had been a number of stand-out moments in the furious, relentless bedlam of working on deck, but perhaps the most powerful was a brief second when I had been pinned against the superstructure of the stern by a pot as it hurtled over the side. This was nothing in the grand scheme of a fisherman's day, a mere inconvenience as one of the pots had been stacked badly (I simply can't think by whom) and had flown off the pile at a strange angle. As I attempted to move out of its way, I had ended up with my back pressed against the frame at the back of *Silver Queen* and had looked up to see the distinctly alarming sight of 15 kilograms of metal leaping off the deck of a speeding fishing boat, being dragged unequivocally in my direction by the several hundred kilograms of pots that were already in the water. The pot clattered mightily into the frame, the line tightened briefly over my legs and for a fraction of a second I was completely helpless, at the mercy of forces so great that flesh and bone could have effortlessly been broken and scattered.

The pot bounced and careered past me before ricocheting off the gunwale and into the sea, leaving me to rub the welt that had appeared on my thighs, shaken at that brief feeling of mortality. It had been utter and entire, with momentum, mass and the ocean combining to render me completely helpless.

* * *

Fishing is an uncompromising business, with the statistics surrounding the industry reading like the aftermath of a battle, a war being raged against the elements and the ocean. It's carnage out there, with any fisherman, even in this enlightened age of Health and Safety, satellite communications and swift evacuation, facing a one-in-twenty chance of being killed during the course of his working life.

Safety has undeniably improved over time, with the Marine Accidents Investigation Branch (MAIB) reporting that in 2010 only 12 fishing vessels were lost around the United Kingdom. That is obviously 12 too many, with each having its own tale of drama and tragedy; however, since 1998 a staggering 321 vessels have either sunk or simply vanished, an average of 23 per year.

Fishing – particularly offshore fishing – involves striking out into a deeply hostile environment in a steel capsule that relies entirely on a clattering collection of pistons and some delicate electronics to keep it pointing vaguely in the right direction, and a thin metal skin to keep it afloat. Once at the fishing grounds, which may well be hundreds of miles offshore, the real work begins, with massive nets, winches, pulleys and hydraulics in constant action on a pitching deck, frequently at night and operated by men close to exhaustion. This is no place for the weak, and yet even in a heavily regulated fleet crewed by fishermen required to have more safety qualifications than ever before, accidents still happen.

In 2010 alone in the UK there were 268 such accidents, including 15 collisions, 10 fires, 25 vessels that flooded or foundered, 182 cases of serious machinery failure and nine men falling overboard. Five fishermen lost their lives. That does not take into account the six who had limbs or portions of limbs amputated, eight who were crushed but survived, three who sustained serious fractures and three who reached dangerous levels of hypothermia.

Once again, go back even a single decade and the statistics become absolutely terrifying. In one year alone, 26 fishermen lost their lives and 115 were seriously injured. Between 1998 and 2010, 165 fishermen were lost.

One might argue, of course, that this is a relatively small number for an entire industry. For example, in the construction industry there were 2,404 deaths between 1976 and 1995; during the same period in fishing there were 454. But it is the size of the workforce that makes the crucial statistical difference and reveals why fishing has long been regarded as the most dangerous profession of them all.

The construction industry provides 4 per cent of all employment in the UK, with a workforce that numbers in the hundreds of thousands. The fishing industry is tiny,

numbering 12,703, including those who fish part-time.

During that 19-year period up to 1995, there were an average of 8.4 deaths per 100,000 workers in the construction industry. In farming, considered by many to be a singularly lethal work environment, there were 9.7 deaths per 100,000 employees over the two years of 2007 and 2008. Extrapolate the figures for the fishing fleet and it becomes 103 deaths per 100,000. In other words, even today a fisherman is 12 times more likely to be killed during the course of his work than someone working on a construction site, and 10 times more likely to be killed than someone on a farm.

To put fish on our plates and to feed the insatiable desire of the markets, there is a battle raging out at sea. It is a constant series of skirmishes, where the conditions may change but the threats are ever present. To slip, to overbalance, to become caught in a bight of rope as it slithers into the sea, these risks are the fisherman's constant companions. They are the demons that lie in wait, biding their time, waiting for that second of inattention. They have an entire lifetime to lay their trap and need only a single moment within that lifetime to spring it.

* * *

As the main road twists along the coast towards the fishing village of Mousehole, it passes a nondescript shed. It perches directly over the sea, this small building with its the foundations laid on sloping rock vanishing into the waves that lap at its very base. A neatly kept garden surrounds it, one that is never left to run riot, tended as it is by the people of the village as a gesture to the memory of the men who left dry land for the last time through the doors that face the sea. It was their last launch, and looking at the shed you can still imagine them gripping tightly onto the lifeboat as it accelerated down the ramp into the darkness, to be gathered into the fury of the night.

I pulled the car up a little distance along the shoreline and walked the last few yards along the pavement. The building is no longer used for the lifeboat, which now sits at a mooring in Newlyn – as tough as a tank and sophisticated as a stealth bomber, a vessel that would have been unrecognizable to the crew of 1981, save for the proud orange livery and, no doubt, the qualities of the people who still man it.

It was early evening and there were a few tourists about, wrapped up warm against the brisk wind that leapt from the bay. I walked slowly up to the monument above the lifeboat shed, the simple carved stone a fitting tribute to the eight men of Penlee. The breeze buffeted and swirled around me, raising untidy white caps in the bay and causing me to hunch my shoulders as I read the inscription. The list of the Penlee crew – Trevelyan Richards, Stephen Madron, Nigel Brockman, John Blewett, Charles Greenhaugh, Kevin Smith, Barrie Torrie and Gary Wallis – is followed by a quote from Winston Churchill: 'The lifeboat drives on with a mercy, which does not quail in the presence of death; it drives on as a proof, a symbol, an affirmation, that man is created in the image of God, and that valour, and virtue, have not perished in the British race.'

I stood for a while studying the names before turning back to the car, parked beside a restless sea that churned and heaved in the wide sweep of the bay.

CHAPTER 6

6 **THE BIG CATCH**

PZ.191

It was tempting to lose myself in the microcosm that is Cadgwith, learning to adapt my daily rhythms to those of the tides and my long-term plans to those of the seasons.

But if I was to learn about the wider picture affecting the boats and men of the cove, it was obvious that I would have to look further afield.

Much as in every small harbour and fishing community around the country, for the Cadgwith men it was not simply a matter of fishing the local waters, looking after their boats and keeping good accounts. There were bigger things going on in the industry over which they had no control, and yet which impacted directly on the success or failure of their particular fishing operation. One of the most prevalent of these was the activity of Britain's larger fishing vessels.

As you would expect, there has always been rivalry between the larger and the smaller vessels. This has worsened over the last decade as fuel prices have increased, margins have become tighter and everyone looks to blame everyone else as business becomes tougher. What is undeniable is that the smaller vessels catch nothing like the amount of fish the larger ones do, with some small-boat skippers viewing the larger fleet as relentless monsters sweeping all from the sea, flooding the markets with too many fish, driving down prices for everyone else and generally ravaging the marine ecosystem.

It is not difficult to see where this attitude might spring from. Through the ages mankind has applied all his fiendish ingenuity to catching fish. Around the world in the 21st century fish are harried, hunted, bombed, poisoned, speared and hooked at a rate and efficiency unmatched throughout history. Recognised techniques for catching fish and shellfish at present include (take a deep breath) beam trawling, demersal otter trawling, multi-rigs, diving, dredging, drift nets, fish-attraction devices, gill nets, tangle nets, trammel nets, handlining, jigging, trolling, hand gathering, harpooning, hydraulic dredging, long lines, pelagic trawling, pole and line, potting, purse seining, seine netting and net traps. On first impressions it seems like a murderous, sustained assault, particularly when you consider that dynamite and cyanide are also used in certain third-world regions.

But there is a real danger in lumping all these techniques and all these vessels together into one vast destructive mob and seeing them as a sort of rampaging task force pillaging the globe. Even in Britain the lines are clearly delineated, with only 8 per cent of our fishing fleet – the vessels over 10 metres in length (the British government's official distinction between 'large' and 'small') – catching 79 per cent of the fish.

The real difference – the heart of the argument that rages even within the fishing community itself – is the differing impact of static and trawled gear. In the simplest possible terms this is the difference between kit that sits in one spot, and equipment that is towed behind a boat, ploughing the seabed or hoovering the blue water of the open sea.

There was only one way for me to find out the real story behind the rivalry between the large and small boats, between the towed and static gear, and that was to

head out to sea on one of the large trawlers. As the port of Newlyn was only a short drive from Cadgwith, this seemed a logical place to seek out a boat. Newlyn is one of the final bastions of large-scale fishing in England and has more registered fishing vessels than any other port in the country – 619 in 2010, of which 75 are over 10 metres long. One of these was called *Billy Rowney* and her skipper kindly agreed to have me on board for what he cheerily described as a week-long 'cruise'.

The skipper in question, Steve Moseley, was a particularly well-regarded figure in Newlyn. Nonetheless I was rather wary of the word 'cruise' being used to describe any commercial fishing trip – a feeling that was reinforced when I mentioned my plan to Nige. He didn't just smile, he roared with laughter.

'Good idea, Mont,' he said, when he had finally calmed down. 'A week on a beam trawler. Yep, that's a great idea. Oh, I can't wait to hear about it after you get back.' For the rest of the day's fishing he would occasionally glance over at me, smile, and then snort with pleasure at the prospect.

Danny Phillips was equally enthralled when I mentioned it to him in the pub.

'Well, hats off to you if you manage it, Monty. You may have to toughen up a bit though – not sure I'd even fancy it myself, to be honest. Still, you obviously know what you're doing.'

He smiled, looking very much like a man talking to someone who plainly didn't know what he was doing. Then he took a sip of his pint, gazing at me over the top of the glass so that all I could make out was the crinkle at the corner of his eyes.

In one of those singularly unhappy coincidences, the week leading up to the trip happened to see the tail end of a hurricane sweeping across the Atlantic.

Great swells thundered across thousands of miles of ocean, getting increasingly annoyed en route until they smashed into Cornwall. The skies overhead were slate grey, all scudding clouds and glowering thunderheads. Off the cliffs of the Lizard all was sound and fury, with gulls shrieking and cawing as they hurtled skywards on buffeting updrafts.

I would lie awake at night, listening to branches thrash against the bedroom windows while rain pelted the panes. With a sick sense of impending doom I looked up the sea conditions on the internet and noted with the sigh of the imminently stricken that the wave heights in the distant fishing grounds off the southwest peninsula were 18 feet. The thought of spending a week out there was absurd, and yet dawn on the day in question saw me miserably packing my bag and eating breakfast (the last food I would keep down for the next 36 hours, as it turned out) before trailing out of the door like a condemned man.

It was only a 40-minute drive to Newlyn. The skies had temporarily cleared, although the wind still buffeted the car as I drove. The sun had crept above an amber horizon as I covered the last mile or so towards the harbour, reflecting in the water that chopped and hissed at the stone walls, making the surface glow like molten metal. It was that beautiful golden hour just after the day has begun, when the deep colours of the land are at their richest. This same light touched the fleet as it sat alongside, enhancing the dark hulls and brightly painted superstructures.

These were no quaint day boats, they were an echo of another era when Britain had a trawler fleet that pushed into frigid Icelandic waters and patrolled the polar fishing grounds. The beam trawlers were

easy to spot, their great arms held aloft towards the blue sky. They looked like huge metallic praying mantises, savagely efficient predators temporarily at rest as their crews scuttled about their decks. There was something implacable about them that made me pause – half in admiration, half in dread – before walking along the jetty towards *Billy Rowney*.

I must have looked particularly forlorn as I trudged into view, something not lost on the skipper, who was watching operations from the bridge wing. He was a stocky, bearded figure who smiled at me reassuringly as he welcomed me alongside.

'Hello there,' he said with a wave, 'you must be Monty. I'm Steve, the skipper. Jump aboard, fella, and let's get your kit stowed.'

'Right,' said Steve, after he had vigorously shaken my hand, 'first things first, you need to meet the guys. Walk this way.'

I followed him to the foredeck, where the three crew members were energetically and noisily manipulating some very large chains attached to some even larger fishing gear. Their work was punctuated by considerable hammering, clanking and – most of all – a great deal of swearing and laughing. They paused as I approached, and then one by one introduced themselves.

The youngest was Jamie Vickers, although at 33 years of age even he was no spring chicken. He was a broad-shouldered, powerful figure and, as is often the way with big men, he seemed surprisingly shy on first introduction. Next was Charlie Downing, who looked positively piratical in a rather dashing Douglas Fairbanks Jr manner – all silver hair and a beaming smile. Finally there was Danny Fisher (a rather good name for a trawlerman, I thought), as lean and hard as the hawsers that snaked across the decks at his feet.

All three of the crew politely enquired about my presence on the trip and offered some tips for the first few days.

'Ah, you'll be fine,' said Danny. 'Just remember when we tell you to move, you move. No questions, no hesitation, when we tell you to get out of the way, it's because something heavy might be imminently arriving and you need to take cover. Do that and you'll be grand.'

> 'The beam trawlers were easy to spot, their great arms held aloft towards the blue sky'

'And can you sing?' asked Charlie. 'Because I do like a sing-song around the gutting table.'

'Gary Barlow,' said Jamie seriously, 'I like a bit of Gary Barlow. But then again that might be because I've been at sea too long.'

Danny offered to show me the bunk space that would be my home for the next week, and having done so left me to unpack my gear below. My bunk was essentially a wooden wardrobe lying on one side, with a ragged curtain that could be pulled across to provide at least a semblance of privacy.

Billy Rowney was kitted out for a crew of seven, although the drastic cuts in crew numbers that are a feature of the modern beam-trawling fleet meant that for this trip only four would be on board, five including myself. In total there were six men who worked this boat, but for every trip that went out two would stay ashore, with everyone taking it in turns to act as crew at sea.

My bunk belonged to one of the crew who was on the shore-based part of the cycle and was plainly something on which he had lavished considerable care and attention – a veritable home from home. He had rigged a small fan halfway down the bunk and had also thoughtfully plastered the walls with pictures of scantily clad ladies. I clambered awkwardly into the bunk space to try it out, noting that every way I turned there was always a shapely woman waving her bikini top at me. This was a most civilised development and I silently congratulated the absent crewman on his splendid taste.

'As a busy fishing harbour in Britain it represented a scene from another age, a ray from the grave of our once great fishing industry'

Even as I lay there I felt the engines of *Billy Rowney* rumble into life beneath me, a deep bass that would be my constant companion for the next eight days. The moment the engines were started the costs of the trip became a critical factor – a large beam trawler will burn about £1000 of diesel in a single day. With the engines turning we were haemorrhaging cash, and for the skipper that meant only one thing – it was time to race to the fishing grounds.

Sure enough, when I moved out onto the open deck, the crew had cast off the ropes and we were already slipping away from the quay. The only way to really look at any fishing port is from the sea and as we moved past the harbour wall I could see the fleet thrown into stark relief against the town behind. As a busy fishing harbour in Britain it represented a scene from another

age, a ray from the grave of our once great fishing industry. Newlyn defiantly retains its identity as a town built around the trawlers, with the fish market dominating the jetty like a great grey hanger. It struck me that no one knows whether the view I had from the stern of *Billy Rowney* on that blustery morning will be the same in ten years' time. Whatever your views on marine conservation may be, there is no denying that the loss of one of our final true fishing ports would strip away something that is key to our national identity. I felt a moment's melancholy as Newlyn faded into the distance, a feeling that deepened considerably as I quietly contemplated the week ahead.

As we moved into the open sea the beat of the engines increased, as did the roll of the hull. I clambered up the near-vertical stairs to the wheelhouse and tapped tentatively on the door.

'Hello, mate,' shouted Steve, 'come on in. Don't be shy.'

He was sprawled in a large chair with his feet up on a great bank of instruments that glowed and beeped impressively before him. The contrast to *Razorbill* – already stark in the sheer dimensions of the vessel – could not have been more marked. We were going hunting and using every piece of modern technology available to help us. Steve saw me peering at the computer screens and flickering lights.

'It's amazing, isn't it?' he said. 'I've no idea what my old man would have made of it all. There's some interesting work being done on just how much of a difference all this stuff makes in terms of how efficiently we fish – in effect how much bang we get for our buck, as it all costs so much money – but nowadays I wouldn't be without it. Same as every other beam-trawler skipper.'

As we chatted Steve patiently talked me

through each screen and keyboard, showing where we were in the ocean to within a few metres, the names and activities of the vessels around us, the topography of the seabed and our planned course for the next few hours. Mixed in with all the delicate electronics were some incongruous, medieval-looking levers.

'For working the beams and hydraulics when we fish,' he said. 'You'll see all of that soon enough.'

'I took a hasty glance at myself in the mirror as I left and saw a hollow-eyed madman, cheeks sallow and expression desperate'

Steve was the most jocular of company, an intelligent man who epitomised the modern generation of trawler skippers. I could have chatted to him all day. However, as *Billy Rowney* pitched, heaved and rolled her way south I abruptly became aware of a light sheen of sweat springing up on my forehead, accompanied by an urge to breathe heavily through my nostrils while staring straight at the horizon. By now I knew the signs well enough and could feel my body preparing to strenuously eject anything internal that wasn't attached, like some sort of errant fleshy pump stuck on overdrive. Steve spotted the imminent crisis at the same time and diplomatically suggested that I go below.

'We'll be steaming for eight hours anyway and there's nothing for you to do during that time. Get your head down – you'll need every bit of sleep you can get over the next week, believe me.'

And so I staggered below, with the boat now slamming and bucking her way through the swells. It seemed to me that she had gone from the benign, protective home in the harbour to something possessed, a charging Valkyrie desperate to enter the carnage of the battle.

Using both hands on the bulkheads I staggered the last few yards to my bunk, rolling into the enclosed space fully clothed to stare at the ceiling inches away from my perspiring forehead. Needless to say I was looking at some vision of beauty peering coquettishly at the camera, and yet all I could focus on was the fact that she was sitting on a lawn as she did so. Dry land. I felt a pang of deep envy.

We would be fishing 60 miles to the southwest of Newlyn and as such were charging into the very heart of the swells that churned the ocean's surface into a series of grey mountains and valleys. I lay in the bunk for the entire duration of the trip, emerging just the once to go for a wee in the boat's tiny toilet. This involved bracing myself against the walls, propping the lid open with one knee and spraying the linoleum of the deck as some fairly elemental forces took charge of operations. I very, very much wanted to be back on *Razorbill*. Or – even better – sitting under a tree anywhere on planet earth.

I had taken some seasickness tablets of positively hallucinogenic strength before boarding. These were prescription drugs designed to stave off nausea for those undergoing chemotherapy – I had decided a week on a beam trawler was no place for half measures – and had the bonus of providing some of the most kaleidoscopic dreams I have ever experienced. In one I was chased up a hill by Bruce Forsyth, who was plainly very annoyed about something and it turns out can really shift for a gentleman of his age. In another I had to play a drum solo at a massive rock concert using only two lumps of cheese. This was not easy, and the solo was something of a disappointment to all. At last, though – after eight hours of fitful sleep – the roar of the engines dropped off to a rumble. We had arrived.

Danny came and shook me awake.

'Up you get, Monty – we're deploying the gear over the side. Something you should take a look at, as this is where it all starts. Besides which you've been on your bunk for hours and I'm worried you'll get bed sores if you stay in much longer.'

I wobbled dutifully to my feet and followed him up the ladder into the narrow companionway where we would prepare to move out onto the deck.

Kitting up meant climbing into my boots, oilskins and life jacket before pulling on thick gloves for the work ahead. Normally this is a relatively straightforward procedure, but on *Billy Rowney* it was to prove to be one of the more emotional parts of the trip. The companionway was narrow and claustrophobic. Along one edge hung the oilskins for the rest of the crew, at least two of whom would always be kitting up the same time as I was. Imagine for a moment three large men in a cupboard trying to get dressed, while the cupboard is being strenuously pushed from side to side by an escaped lunatic. Then picture at least two of the men smoking, while the third tries his best to avoid the glowing tips of the cigarettes as they periodically swoop past. If you add the fact that the companionway was invariably warm and fuggy, with that special smell that can only be created by confining several large, sweaty, flatulent men in a steel capsule at sea for a week, you have something approaching an idea of the

atmosphere that was to be the launch point for every haul.

I had nothing like the sea legs of the other crew members, of course. They were positively elegant in their movements, balancing effortlessly as they slipped into their boots or shrugged into a life jacket, dancers rolling to the rhythm of the sea. I on the other hand looked as though I was performing some sort of inebriated hoedown as I hopped past the doorway with one foot in a wellie and the other wiggling optimistically in mid-air. Such exertion left me hot, bothered and feeling desperately seasick.

But as the week progressed there was to be one other special – very special – factor about the corridor of doom. For me this single feature vastly increased the sliding scale of horror, shifting things all the way from the 'mildly unpleasant' end, straight across to 'deepest pit of gloomy death'. This feature was the toilet.

Just off the companionway was the loo – the only one on board – the door of which was permanently latched open. The toilet was small and, despite everyone's valiant attempts to keep it clean, it was nonetheless subjected to the energetic attention of a crew who ate well and often, and had alimentary canals that were plainly in tip-top condition. Over the course of the week the smell coming from this tiny cubicle became apocalyptic, to such a degree that I developed a slight concern that if I left my wellies too close to the door they might melt. As I bounced from wall to wall while kitting up, I always had one wide eye on the entrance to the toilet. I was mesmerised by the thought of pitching through the door and clattering into the porcelain, all the while holding my breath, feet skittering on the lino as I tried to accelerate away from the horrors of the bowl.

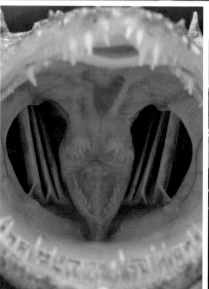

The first kitting-up session was soon over, with the crew opening the side doors of the companionway to drop elegantly onto the deck. They left behind a man gripped by waves of nausea, with his life jacket on backwards and his wellies on the wrong feet, hanging onto one of the hooks and muttering darkly at the misery of it all. I stumbled out into a black Atlantic night and weaved my way forward to collapse under the covered forward section of the boat, known as the whaleback. Here, from a prone position slumped against a hatch, I watched the crew swing into action and the beam-trawling operation commence.

Beam trawling is precisely what it sounds like – two massive metal beams are pulled across the seabed, with a network of chains trailing along behind them. The idea is that the great weight of the beam – six tons each side – keeps the gear on or close to the sea floor, while the chains cause any creatures living there to lift upwards as they approach. Directly above and behind the onrushing beam is the open mouth of the net, which funnels the fish (and anything else that happens to live out its life cycle on the ocean floor) into the end. This is known as the cod end and is the part that is lifted back onto the deck throughout fishing operations over the course of the week.

Even in my befuddled state I could see that deploying gear this weighty was an extremely dangerous part of the process. It was also obvious that the crew were highly skilled, moving quickly from vast shackle to lumpen bolt as the beams were lifted into the air above them. Working on a canted factory floor, as a jet-black ocean hissed and snarled only yards away, they carefully guided six tons of clanking, swaying metal over each side. An air of quiet competence pervaded the entire scene, with never a voice raised nor a harsh word exchanged.

Soon both beams were trailing in the water on either side of the hull and, on a signal from Charlie to the wheelhouse (a final shout of 'Gear's away, Steve', which came across as 'Gashhewahstef' in the mayhem of the night), the pulleys overhead whined and spun, and the trawl vanished beneath the surface, the great spools of the hawsers unravelling for several minutes until the gear was bumping across the seabed 300 feet beneath. And there it would stay for the next eight days, lifted only every three hours for a few minutes at a time so that the cod ends could be emptied on deck. *Billy Rowney* was a fishing machine and for the next week it would go about its business with a constant and unrelenting application.

The great weight of the trawl dragged hundreds of feet below our churning wake acted as a colossal pair of stabilisers that deadened the roll of the boat. This fact was not lost on the bright yellow figure now curled beneath the gutting table, who looked up with sudden hope as the deck steadied beneath him.

Perhaps I might survive after all. Perhaps I wouldn't be lifted off *Billy Rowney* by a helicopter in two days, swaying on the winch like a boneless bag of meat, pawing deliriously at my own face and calling feebly for my mother.

'That's it for now, Monty,' said Charlie kindly, leaning over me with his hands on his knees, 'you can go back down below and kip for a few hours, as we don't haul for a wee while yet. I'll give you a shake when it's time to come back on deck.'

I crawled back to the corridor of doom, shrugging out of my oilskins to tumble down the stairs, creep across the carpet of the cabin and climb into my bunk like some aging Labrador clambering onto a sofa. I remained fully clothed and simply

'For the next eight days, no one aboard Billy Rowney would sleep for more than four hours in a single stretch' pulled my sleeping bag over my head with a muttered 'Bloody hell'. I was keenly aware that although one trip out onto the deck was over, there were – for me personally – approximately 35 to go. This was not a comforting thought.

The crew of *Billy Rowney* would now switch into a well-established routine. All would be centred around the two cod ends – one either side – being recovered onto the boat, lifted over the low gunwales to spew their catch onto the battered wooden decking. This would happen every three hours for the next eight days, and the four crew members needed to eat, sleep and conduct their lives entirely around the tyranny of this unrelenting cycle. At any one time there always had to be a crew member on watch on the bridge, and for every haul there would be two men on deck. Each haul would take at least an hour to process. Steve, as the skipper, would work longer shifts on watch and appear on the deck only in the event of a drama or when all hands were required.

The standard routine for any crew member would be three hauls in a row – which equates to six hours with only snatched moments of rest. There would then follow a break of a single haul – allowing six hours to perform basic tasks around the boat, eat and get what sleep they could. In the midst of this 12-hour stretch, each crew member also had to take a two-hour watch on the bridge, allowing the skipper to have a break so he too could get some sleep. In essence this meant that for the next eight days, no one aboard *Billy Rowney* would sleep for more than four hours in a single stretch.

For the crew member of a trawler, working life is quite unlike any other profession in Britain. As I lay in my bunk, rolling from side to side with elbows braced, fighting the waves of nausea, the only thing I could really equate it to was the life of a high-altitude mountaineer. There is sickness – well, there certainly was in my case – sleep deprivation, a brutally hostile environment, physical exhaustion and the constant lurking spectre of death or injury should you drop your guard.

Such cheery thoughts saw me drift off into rather miserable sleep, only to be woken two hours later by Danny.

'Up you get, Monty, time to do the first haul. There's a cuppa up top for you, then it's time you did some work.' He looked nauseatingly cheerful – an invincible trawlerman about to set about his business.

This was something of a seminal moment for me. It would have been the easiest thing in the world to stay in the bunk, that wonderful, dark, womb-like space embraced by the heartbeat of the engines. I was not a crew member, I was along on the trip as a guest and observer, and what's more I felt absolutely terrible – surely everyone would understand if I stayed put and popped out on deck when I was feeling slightly more civilised? But something – I've no idea what – drove me up the ladder and into the fug of the galley.

'Aha, here he is, risen from the grave,' said Jamie.

'Bout time too,' said Danny, cigarette smouldering, 'I was getting worried about that deep vein thrombosis people get on aeroplanes. Can be very serious, that.'

He handed me my tea in a cup which I couldn't help noticing had the word 'Twat' emblazoned on it in large blue letters.

'There you go, Mont, you even get your own special mug,' he said with a smile and a conspiratorial wink. He was plainly a nice man, as was Jamie, but I genuinely didn't care. I wanted them to go away. In fact I wanted it all to go away. I took a long slug of tea before gingerly placing the cup back on the tilting table and walking stiffly out into the corridor of doom. Gripping the wood of the doorway with white knuckles, I managed to get my feet into both wellies and pull my oilskins on before standing up to sway helplessly while staring straight ahead. This coincided with the engine revs dropping slightly – a signal, it seemed, for the crew to spring into action.

'Right,' said Danny as he bustled past me, 'I'm going to keep an eye on you out there. You stay back for now, stand where we tell you and we'll process this haul. There's plenty more for you to do later.'

'I felt intensely vulnerable, far from home in this steel capsule, in the dead of night, in a great ocean, entirely out of my depth'

With that he threw the door open and stepped out into the night on the port side, with Jamie moving onto the starboard deck at the same time. I stepped out behind him and moved quickly forward so I could watch operations from beneath the safety of the whaleback.

By now it was late at night and our entire world was represented by the pool of light cast by powerful lamps set high in the superstructure. Beyond was inky darkness where only the occasional wave crest would appear, crackling and roaring like some angry wraith before melting away into the deep black of the Atlantic. There was no horizon, no point of reference, simply the hawsers vibrating with tension as they broke the surface of the sea, spray

shattering and spinning from them in bright droplets, and a constant bass backing track of the engines offset by the high whine of the winches.

The deck pitched and rolled beneath my feet, making standing still extremely difficult, and all the while the sea hissed along the hull, biding its time and awaiting its chance. I felt intensely vulnerable, far from home in this steel capsule, in the dead of night, in a great ocean, entirely out of my depth.

Abruptly the massive chains connecting the hawsers to the beams themselves broke the surface, the nets beneath showing as an immense dark green cloud just beneath the water's surface. The winches changed their tone, as the lighter cod ends were lifted out of the sea to swing on board and hover over the deck, heavy with the catch, water pouring from the mesh to sluice into the scuppers.

Danny and Jamie moved quickly beneath each net, hauling on a bright orange knot at their base. With three or four educated tugs, the net sprang open to release its catch onto the deck, an avalanche of marine life that skittered and sprawled across the planking in a living tide.

I had mentally prepared myself for this first haul, knowing that I would be shocked by the scale of it. As a man used to the gentle progress of *Razorbill* and the sustainable operations of the smaller boats, this pile of marine life before me represented several days' fishing effort for the entire Cadgwith fleet. What I was looking at was one haul – there would be at least 50 more over the course of this week, and there were many other boats working these same waters. I stepped forward slightly and squatted next to the haul to study the catch more closely. Each of *Billy Rowney*'s beams was about the same width

as a telegraph pole, and the catch from this single trawl represented a cross-section of marine life from every level of the food chain close to the sea floor – starfish, sponges, octopus, crabs, lobsters and fish.

The ones that really drew the eye were the monkfish. This was one of the primary target species of the trip, and the haul heaved with their gigantic grey forms. A few of them were real monsters, three to four feet long, gaping and snapping their mouths as they thrashed on the deck.

Slithering through the haul were two or three large conger eels, their reptilian forms spinning and writhing amid the chaos. Haddock thrashed in their death throes, with scores of megrim sole flipping and twitching throughout the catch. The latter was another target species of the trawl, a creature not found close to shore and highly desirable for the overseas markets. Two large cod gasped at the edge of the catch, their lives pointlessly lost in the face of complex legislation. I saw Danny move to lift one of them over the side into the sea, grunting with effort as he did so. He glanced at me as I watched, and gave a small shake of his head in disgust. The quota system – the one topic that seems to dominate the thoughts of any modern fisherman – applied in this environment more than any other.

But therein lay the dilemma of this form of fishing. Initially the arguments seem simple enough, neatly encapsulated by the seething pile of marine life before me. Surely carving a groove in the sea floor – up to eight centimetres deep according to a recent study – represents total destruction of a delicate marine environment, ravaging the source of so much of the protein for the waters above and essentially undermining the foundation of the food chain? As I looked at this clicking,

writhing, squirming mass of marine life, there it was writ large – destruction and death. And yet, as ever, the reality is considerably more complex.

There has been a great deal of work done on the impacts of beam trawling and, although the negative effect of ploughing the seabed may seem obvious, many of the studies have turned up contradictory results. The consensus of opinion seems to be that the real impact of beam trawling swings on two main factors: how often an area is trawled and the composition of the seabed itself.

An area that has been beam trawled will take about five years to return to its original state, with some long-lived, slow-growing and non-mobile organisms such as sponges and bivalves not returning to their original abundance for eight years after a single trawl. Sadly most areas where the trawlers operate don't have anything like this period to recover – some regions in heavily fished zones such as the Irish Sea are trawled as often as four times a year.

Studies seem to suggest that these areas of seabed have a great many smaller fish, as well as a loss of diversity – so there are fewer species than would be present in a natural system. Many species disappear completely, which may have a knock-on effect higher up the food chain. Large, slow-growing fish are similarly affected, with frequent trawling seeing a decrease in their abundance and average size. Opportunistic animals such as hermit crabs will flourish as they move into what is essentially a recently ravaged furrow of dead and dying species that represent a carrion bonanza.

For me there was one study that stood out, one dry scientific paper that perfectly illustrated the grave issues created by industrial-scale fishing when it is allied

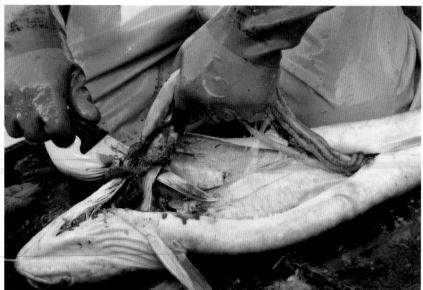

with a system of fish quotas. This is not a problem created by the fishermen alone. It is created by bureaucrats, by legislation that demands fish are shovelled overboard to honour figures and regulations that make perfect sense in Europe's distant corridors of power, but have seen many fishermen forced out of business as they watch their catch twist and sink in their wake, food for the gulls and the scavengers that click and claw their way over the seabed beneath.

Between 2002 and 2005, data was collected from 3,643 hauls taking place on 142 trawlers, working in the English Channel, the Western Approaches, the Celtic Sea and the Irish Sea. For every year of the study, an estimated 186 million fish and cephalopods – octopus, squid and cuttlefish – were caught. Of these, 117 million were thrown overboard, with 58 per cent of these discards taking place from beam trawlers. In a world desperate for protein, this surely represents a criminal waste of a valuable resource, an avalanche of food sinking to the sea floor to rot in the darkness. Strip away the science and the economics and we are left with mankind at his most wantonly destructive. Whether you view it as a fisherman trying to make a living or as a conservationist trying to preserve an ecosystem, it is enough to make you weep.

I began to shovel the catch through the scuppers and over the side. Only about a third of a modern beam trawler's catch is marketable, and in some areas that figure can drop to as little as 5 per cent. The rest is inevitable collateral damage. In the darkness off the stern I could hear the shrieks of gulls as they squabbled and fed, the first stage of a new food chain living off the wake of the great steel vessels that now rumbled through their world.

As I worked on the discards, Danny and Jamie set about gutting the catch. Bracing their feet against the roll of the deck, they lifted each fish off the table and made a small incision, removing the guts with a flick of the wrist. All the while they chatted amiably, their hands moving entirely independently, muscle memory taking charge in a repetitive motion that took place at bewildering speed. Soon the catch was gutted and washed, before the final stage of being lowered into the cold store under the deck. The entire process had taken about an hour, a seamless model of efficiency and effort.

By now I was beginning to feel slightly more human, although any sudden movements resulted in a sharp intake of breath and a wave of nausea that in turn caused me to mutter darkly to myself and stare grimly into the middle distance. As Danny and I took off our oilskins in the corridor, I was just coherent enough to chat, albeit in short, staccato phrases while studiously avoiding looking at the toilet.

'Danny, you've been doing this all your working life. What do you think when people criticise beam trawling as being unsustainable?'

Danny paused for a moment before answering, moving through to the saloon to flick on the kettle as he spoke.

'Look, I know it's complicated and all that, but really what is the difference between a trawlerman and a farmer who ploughs a field? We are essentially ploughing the seabed for food – of course it has an impact. But if a farmer didn't plough his land, there'd be lovely forests everywhere.'

He rolled a cigarette as he spoke, lighting it so the end glowed as he inhaled. He paused and studied the tip. 'We get so much stick as fishermen, but we're

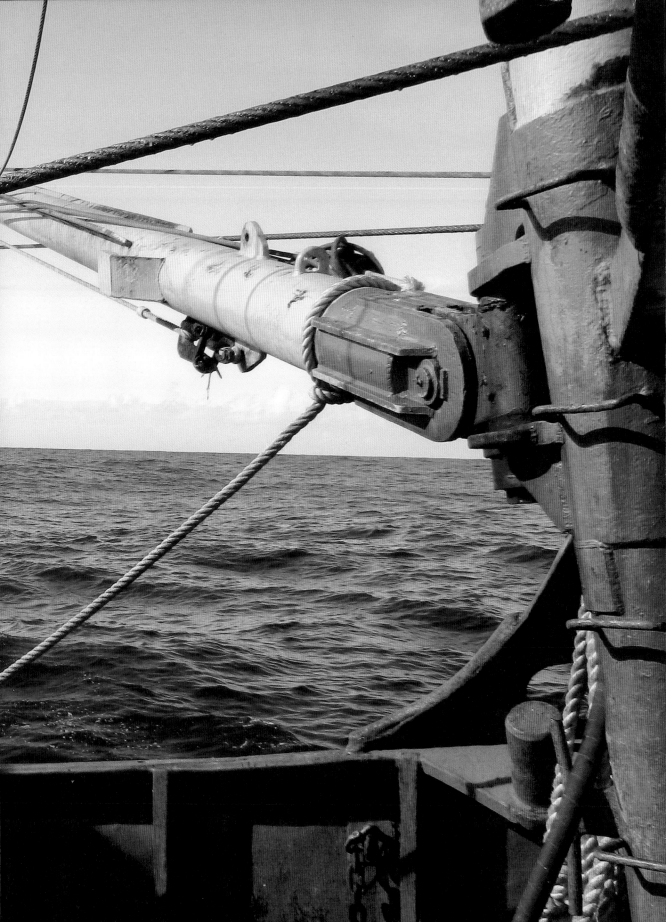

only working within the rules – and believe me if we didn't have to chuck so much of our catch overboard we'd be out here half of the time and covering a lot less ground.'

Steve had come down from the bridge, with Jamie taking a watch in his place, and spoke up from behind me as he entered the saloon.

'All of this will become theoretical fairly soon anyway, Monty.' He smiled rather grimly as he spoke. 'If diesel prices keep going up, there'll be no large fishing boats working out of Cornwall within a few years. The question then, of course, is where will we get our fish from? Overseas, probably, although that doesn't seem to be something a lot of people ask themselves when they are getting stuck into the trawlers.'

'I crawled out of my bunk and climbed into the fetid corridor to begin another haul'

This may not be as far-fetched as it seems. You only had to chat to Danny for a second to realise that this was no Cornish boy – 'For fook's sake...' being the intro to most conversations. Here was a proud Lancastrian, hailing from Fleetwood – up until 20 years ago one of the largest fishing ports in the country.

'It all just vanished,' he said, when I asked him about his heady days working on the great trawlers. 'It was unthinkable, the whole place was based around the fishing fleet and within three or four years they all just disappeared. The town died, simple as that. And now I'm here.'

Jamie's story was similar, a Grimsby lad driven south by harsh economic reality.

'I'm a fisherman,' he told me. 'My dad was a fisherman, and his before him. I'm proud of what I do. When I look into the future, though, there doesn't seem to be much hope. I wonder what my lad will end up doing, but right now I'm not sure I'd even want him in the business, it's so difficult to predict if it has a future.'

'It's been a double whammy, really,' said Steve. 'We might have been able to deal with quotas. And we might have been able to deal with the massive increase in the price of diesel. But trying to cope with both of those at the same time ... well, we're pretty knackered unless something changes fairly soon.'

This was a fascinating discussion, but by now the familiar sweat had broken out on my forehead and I was beginning to yawn. I excused myself and slipped through the hatch that led down into the sleeping berths, vanishing like a rat down a drainpipe.

It was – surely – only seconds later that Charlie was shaking me awake. Convinced that this must be some sinister initiation ritual, I glanced at my watch to see that it was indeed 3 a.m. and I had been unconscious for two hours. I crawled out of my bunk and climbed into the fetid corridor to begin another haul. Jamie was once again on deck duty, although this time he was accompanied by Charlie, who gave me a big smile and a cheery wave.

'My God, it moves and even stands upright every now and then. I know just what you need to cheer you up, Mont. Just the thing, just the thing. Stick with me on this haul and I'll sort you out right enough.'

Moments later we were standing on the deck as the cod end swung into view. The weather had worsened, with the boat bucking and heaving in the darkness, making it feel in one moment as if I was weightless and the next pressing me deep into the hull so my knees almost buckled. The wind swirled and twisted around the deck, tugging at my oilskins and buffeting my face. It smelled entirely of the sea without even a trace of dry land, the breath of the ocean far from shore.

Charlie had moved beneath the cod end, tugged the stopper knot open and then quickly jumped back as the avalanche of fish spread glittering and heaving under the deck lights. He held the cod end open and gestured me over.

'Right, Mont, in you get. We clear the cod end out every haul and it looks like just the job for a man of your calibre.'

And climb in I did. Next time you feel sick, or have a hangover, or haven't eaten for a day or so, I can recommend a cure. Try clambering into a man-sized cave of wet and slimy mesh that is still sluicing cold Atlantic sea water, all the while skidding on a pile of snapping monkfish and irate conger eels, reaching up over your head to grab furious crabs and flapping flatfish that have become stuck in the more dingy recesses of the constricted end. You emerge a new man, let me tell you.

It's nice to have a little job, one that makes you feel useful, and this was to become something of a speciality for me over the next week. For some reason best known to the god of random things, when it comes to clearing out a bunged-up cod end, it turns out I have a bit of a natural gift. I staggered back to the saloon feeling rather pleased with myself. I had done two hauls. There were 34 to go.

And so the week passed, a series of shakes in the small hours, accompanied by the steady and inexorable creep of exhaustion. There was also, I'm pleased to say, the glorious return of my appetite. This occurred in earnest on the third day and saw me ravage the galley like some rabid predator. Danny was delighted and clapped me on the back as he cooked up a vast breakfast.

'One egg or two, Monty?' he asked as he skated towards me on a wildly canting galley floor, a frying pan held before him that brimmed with boiling, spitting fat.

'Ermmm, just the one, thanks, Danny,' I said as I backed into a bulkhead. 'Any more than that and you'll set the boat – or yourself – on fire, won't you?'

'Fook off,' he said cheerily, turning back to his work.

Sleeping for only two or three hours at a stretch does strange things to a person. There is the gradual, insipid onset of fatigue, quietly weighing down the limbs and dulling the senses. It was rather like becoming steadily drunk over a week, until towards the end I had turned into something of a burbling wretch. The days and nights blurred into one, with each 24 hours broken into a series of hauls, interspersed with trudges back to the bunk and the periodic intake of vast quantities of food to fuel the physiological furnace that burned steadily throughout.

Gradually, under the patient tutelage of the crew, my efficiency on deck increased. As the days passed I learned how to work at the gutting table, wash down the catch and shovel ice below decks in the cold store. This was filling with box after box of fish, hundreds and hundreds of kilograms of prime seafood, most of it destined for the European markets. We were still heaving massive cod over the side though – the crew shaking their heads and staring venomously into the middle distance as they did so – fishermen throwing their greatest prize, and much of their living, overboard.

I was delighted to be able to help the crew in their work, even in a small way. I may have had reservations about the fishing method and was seeing with my own eyes the amount of the catch that went back into the sea, but there was no denying the decency of the men who worked around me.

Soon we were in the second half of the trip, the homeward leg in terms of shifts and sleep deprivation. I made a list of things I was looking forward to when the trip ended, reciting it sotto voce to myself on deck as the wind howled and the waves roared. Even Jamie had to admit that it was getting a tad blowy.

'A bit poor, I suppose you could say,' he said, when I questioned him about it. 'Hmmm, definitely a bit poor.'

'The waves looked mountainous to me, even more so at night when they appeared out of the veil of darkness'

It turned out that we were now fishing in a Force Seven, occasionally gusting Force Eight. The waves looked mountainous to me, even more so at night when they appeared out of the veil of darkness, shifting walls of water bearing down on our stern as we churned our way onwards. At some level I suppose it made me happy to know that I was experiencing reasonably intense conditions, but at every other level it just seemed to make life immeasurably harder. Lifting a basket of fish from one place to another involved a series of giant slow-motion steps as the boat rolled in one direction, followed by a further series of extremely rapid tiny ones going the same way as it rolled the other. I would stagger in

and out of vision when required to move anything heavy, attempting to put it down in the right place before being steered violently in the wrong direction by the force of gravity. This frequently went on for several minutes, much to the amusement of the crew.

And slowly – as the week crept past – the fish hold filled, with box after box being lowered into the maw of the hatch to be iced and stacked in steep towers. Steve called me to the wheelhouse after one shift and announced that, due to the conditions, we'd have to stay out for at least another week. Seeing my crestfallen expression, he laughed delightedly.

'Only joking, fella, probably heading back in the day after tomorrow. Hang on in there – you've actually become moderately useful. Only 48 hours to go and then we'll have you back home to your mum.'

I skipped back down the ladder, a new man. Over the next day or so the weather even began to settle and although I could never honestly say that I enjoyed the work – there was just too much death and waste before me for that – I found new energy and strength in the proximity of its conclusion.

It was with a genuine sense of unreality that I found myself out on deck preparing for the final haul. As the cod end spewed its contents onto the deck, I scrambled inside for one last time. This euphoric moment was somewhat tempered by Jamie attempting to re-tie the end while I was still in it, resulting in a remarkably athletic exit on my part involving much flapping of oilskins and skidding of wellies. I was banished once again to the protection of the whaleback as the beams came back on board, their deadly work done for another trip. This was no place for the novice, and Steve had earlier shown me the stump of

'The market's insatiable desire
for fish in vast quantities
demands that the beam trawlers
continue to work the sea floor'

his forefinger to illustrate the folly of overconfidence on a first trip.

'Thought I knew what I was doing,' he mused. 'Plainly, I didn't.'

Once again the crew swarmed over the gear as it swung in lethal, weighty arcs, shackling the beast before it could do any damage. Finally subdued by massive chains that tied it alongside, the winches overhead whined into life for one last time to heave the gear on board. The moment it swung over the side, landing on the deck with a tectonic boom that made the entire vessel resonate, the roll of the boat changed. Freed from the drag of the trawl, *Billy Rowney* came alive, kicking her heels and tossing her bow as she turned for home. Coincidentally the same scene was being repeated by her new crew member on deck, causing Jamie to laugh out loud as I walked jauntily past him.

'That's the biggest smile I've seen all week. Someone's pleased to be going home. Mind you, I'm sure there's a crew berth available next trip if you fancy it.'

Even though it was made in jest, I briefly considered the implications of his offer, before shaking my head with a weary grin. I was exhausted, so tired that my left hand had started to shake slightly like that of a hungover vicar. I felt ravaged by interrupted sleep patterns and the unrelenting nature of the work. I wasn't entirely sure when I had last changed my pants, or indeed brushed my teeth. All of this despite the fact that I had accumulated more time in my bunk than any other crew member, as I had (happily) not been qualified to undertake the watch-keeping duties on the bridge, performed by everyone else as part of their normal shift pattern. In terms of a first outing as a proper crewman, I couldn't help feeling that I was definitely in the 'mattress-loving-simpering-lightweight' category, as opposed to the much desired 'man-of-steel-wouldn't-fancy-taking-him-on-in-a-brawl' one.

There was no denying the impact we had wrought on the seabed we were leaving behind us. In demanding seafood in such quantities, we create a real dilemma for the fishing and environmental lobbies. In the United Kingdom an estimated 94 per cent of the demersal catch – the bottom-dwellers such as flatfish and monkfish – comes from only 4 per cent of the boats, mainly consisting of the beam- and otter-trawling fleet. In ordering that succulent plaice or delicate sole in a restaurant, we all become culpable in this form of fishing. On the one hand this keeps the industry alive and ensures that men such as Danny, Jamie, Charlie and Steve continue to ply their trade as trawlermen. This is a good thing, a great thing, as one of the lingering impressions of my time on board was the quality of the crew and their deep pride in their profession and heritage. In addition to this direct employment, a recent study estimated that for every job at sea there are four created ashore, and so the crew of *Billy Rowney* were a well-head of work for those left behind, their efforts not only putting money in their own pockets but acting as the very lifeblood of communities such as Newlyn.

Of course the flip side of this is the sustainability issue. Should we really be ploughing a furrow in the seabed to feed ourselves? Should we be shovelling a heaving, gasping, doomed harvest back overboard? Are there alternative means of fishing on this scale that do not leave such carnage in their wake? Research is ongoing, with various alternative techniques being trialled with limited success. At present, the market's insatiable desire for fish in vast quantities demands that the beam trawlers continue to work the sea floor, weaving their patterns in the darkness far offshore as the gulls clamour and squabble in their wake.

* * *

My return to Cadgwith coincided with a fine, clear afternoon that gave way to a gorgeous evening. It was wonderful to be back, and having strolled through the boats on the beach – the skippers long since headed home at the end of the day's fishing – I mysteriously found myself on the Stick some time later sipping a pint. One of the things I had learned to treasure since coming to Cadgwith was the slow passage of time, with the track of the day measured by the tide, and the activities of the fishermen dictated by the movement of their quarry in the restless waters of the fishing grounds. This was a stark contrast to the industry of *Billy Rowney* and I relished the cathedral hush of the scene around me.

I had arrived in the village with a clear idea of the importance of conservation, of the need to monitor the activities of the fishing fleet around our coast. Working with Nige and the other skippers had not faded that vision, but now it was tempered by the reality of having had an experience of life on the beam trawler. I had been given a glimpse of the front line of fishing, and it seemed to me to be a place where the landscape was churned by bureaucratic barrages and the way ahead fogged by uncertainty.

There is, of course, a place for the larger fishing vessels. But the risks of unfettered fishing activity are abundantly clear, with mankind's history littered with an obstinate denial of vanishing fish stocks. Personally I retained enough faith in human nature to believe that many of the

rules and regulations had been introduced in good faith, genuinely motivated by conservation and valiant attempts to secure the future of the industry.

But as I looked out on the Cadgwith fleet in the gathering gloom, it seemed to me that there must be a better way to regulate, to communicate with the fishermen and to utilise generations of knowledge. With certain conservation measures creating nets that catch ever-smaller fish, and quotas that see much of the catch tossed overboard by men despairing of their livelihood, there must surely be another way forward.

It is undeniable that many of the problems we face today have been created by the fishing industry's standard response to low prices and disappearing stocks – to use larger vessels that catch vast amounts of fish, scouring the oceans ever further afield. But perhaps the answer lies in reverting to a more traditional model, using small boats to supply local communities directly? There were well-documented stories of programmes like this around the world, schemes recently adopted by inshore fishing fleets facing their own demise and now operating with varying levels of success. One of the most famous was on the other side of the Atlantic, offering what just might be a ray of hope in an otherwise unremittingly bleak future.

There was nothing for it. Nige and I had to go to America.

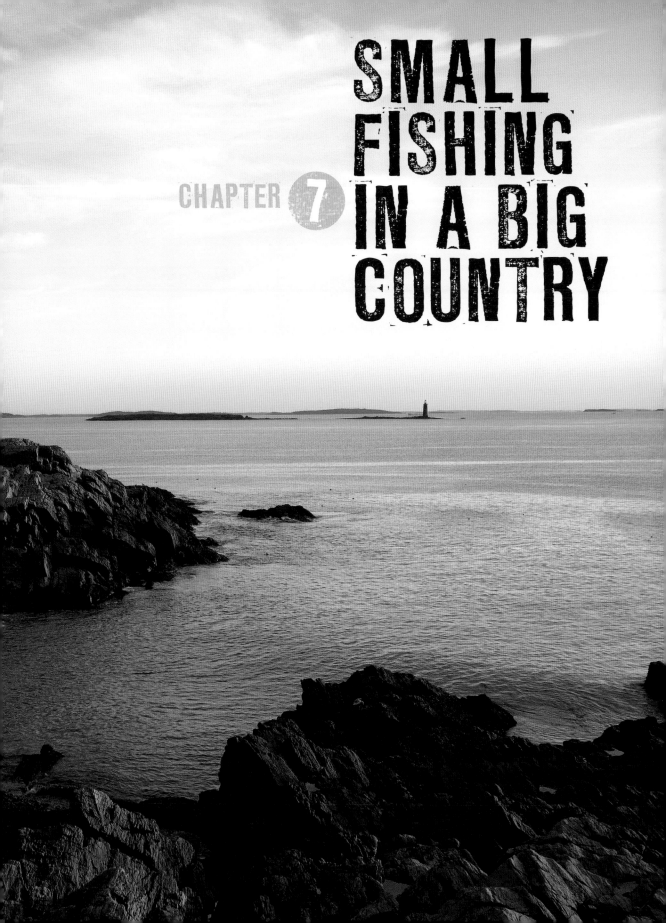

CHAPTER 7

SMALL FISHING IN A BIG COUNTRY

It was very odd indeed to see Nige standing at the counter of a coffee shop in Heathrow Airport.

It was an incongruous setting for a man I was so used to seeing with the sea at his back. He was wearing his smart blue jumper, the RNLI logo emblazoned on the front in deep red text. With his earring and stubble he looked rather like a rock star heading off on tour. He smiled as I hove into view carrying a colossal set of bags.

'Ah, Monts,' he said, bustling forward to help me, 'nice to see you. Roight on.'

'Morning, Nige,' I said. 'Ready to go?'

'I am, I am,' he replied, brandishing a smart new passport as he spoke. 'Had to order one of these, though. Can't get out of Cornwall without it, you see.'

Nige had not done a great deal of flying in his life; in fact he had flown only once before – to Tenerife for a week's holiday. But as I watched him pass through the hectic airport, it struck me how relaxed he was. Perhaps this was because his working life consisted of dealing with the unexpected every day, of constantly adapting to shifts in the environment around him. A small-boat fisherman develops a tremendous – and well-founded – sense of his own self-reliance. For Nige this seemed to be just another trip out, albeit one at 600 knots through swirling currents of wind around outcrops of cloud. Any snags, it seemed, could be dealt with using a few bits of masking tape, some old line and possibly a call to Tonks to come and tow us in.

There was one slight moment of chagrin. As we settled in our tiny seats on the aircraft, the intercom crackled into life and the captain welcomed us aboard. The voice was calm, measured and entirely in control. It was also female. Nige glanced across at me with a single raised eyebrow.

'A lady skipper, eh?' He settled back into his seat and looked rather thoughtful. I made a mental note not to mention rabbits or to order a pasty.

During the flight itself, the only incident of any note was that Nige and I had to share the arm-rest between us. I wanted the journey to be as pleasant as possible for him and so conceded ownership, allowing him to plant one elbow and get comfortable. Sadly the elbow in question was directly and consistently on the volume button of the film I was trying to watch, which experienced an aural rollercoaster of being very loud indeed, then very quiet, then very loud, then very quiet again. After an hour, ears ringing, I gave up. This was just as well, as Nige's elbow had by now shifted to the channel button, so I would have ended up watching a cartoon anyway.

It was late in the afternoon by the time we arrived in Boston Airport, where we were to pick up our hire car for the last section of the journey up the coast. The vehicle was massive, looking like a colossal four-wheel-drive hearse with tinted windows. It was very much the sort of vehicle that a pimp would drive, or possibly a gangster with no taste. Inside it was essentially a sitting room on wheels and Nige beamed as he settled into the overly upholstered passenger seat.

'I should get one of these for taking bait down to the cove, Mont,' he said approvingly.

The drive up the coast was breathtaking. Sadly the highlight was not the gorgeous autumnal hues of the ancient Maine

woodland through which we passed; it was the fact that we figured out you could add your own voice to the recordings in the vehicle's satellite-navigation system. To the next person to hire that vehicle, I apologise. As they approach the first corner an electronic shout of 'Turn right, you daft bugger' will echo out of the dashboard in broadest Cornish, which I imagine may lead to some sort of lawsuit. Nige found this very, very funny indeed, as did I, and our progress up the coast was punctuated with roars of laughter and a certain amount of erratic weaving across the white line in the centre of the road.

Day passed into night, although happily this coincided with our arrival in Port Clyde, our first stop on a four-day voyage of discovery. We settled in to our hotel – a beautiful old clapperboard building straight out of a Salinger novel – and lapsed into jet-lagged oblivion.

The next morning revealed a charming little fishing cove, complete with a faded wooden jetty that meandered towards the horizon. Thick deciduous forests coated a shoreline of rocky inlets, with the occasional house tucked discreetly into a quiet glade. The water in the harbour was completely still, reflecting a red dawn as it murmured and rustled around the pillars of the pier. It was quite, quite beautiful. An American flag hung limply on a pole by the water's edge, tattered and torn by a hundred winds that had shrieked and howled off the bay, a stark contrast to the gentle sea breeze of today.

Eager to go off exploring, I ambled over to Nige's room to find him and made the moderately alarming discovery that he had gone. For some reason I had decided that this extraordinarily capable man would be helpless in any environment outside the cove and had visions of finding him wandering around outside in his underpants being attacked by crows. I should have known better, and on rushing down to the small cafe on the shore found him happily chatting away to several of the local fishermen. Pausing at the door, I took a moment to study the scene.

Fishermen the world over share certain characteristics. They are highly independent and yet rely very much on a communal approach to the hazards they face at sea. Physically they look similar – lean, weathered and tough. But for me it is the eyes that really allow you to identify a full-time fisherman. Peering at a distant horizon all your working life creates a certain something – a steady, measured gaze that quietly assesses the situation ahead. I suppose it would be too much to say that one fisherman can spot another by this feature alone, but it epitomised every man of the sea I had ever met on my travels. It is the look of a hunter, a final echo of our distant past.

Whether it was this characteristic that had allowed the local fishermen to spot Nige among them (my rather fanciful notion), or a fanatical and shared love of a large cup of coffee (probably slightly more realistic), nonetheless he was happily chatting away to a large group. They were nodding vigorously as he spoke, occasionally laughing at a shared experience. Seeing me enter the cafe, he waved me over.

'Morning, Monts,' he said with a broad smile, peering over the top of a coffee cup the size of a milk churn. 'Just been introducing myself to the local fellas. This is Gary.'

Gary, a large man in a checked shirt and peaked cap, nodded in my direction.

'Knew he was a fisherman the moment he walked in,' he said in a distinct New

England drawl. 'It's the hands.'

Aha, the hands, I thought.

He glanced down at my hands. 'And what do you do?' he asked.

* * *

By a happy coincidence, Gary was a central figure in the fishery we had come to investigate. As we chatted over yet more coffee, warm in the fug of the shop, he talked of the problems facing the fishing fleets locally. We were separated from Cadgwith by several thousand miles of cold Atlantic water, centuries of history and the development of a different culture, and yet as the conversation developed I realised we could just as well have been sitting at the bar of the Cadgwith Cove Inn.

'The fishermen had taken charge of their own destiny'

'Our lobster fleet is doing all right, but the small finfish boats – basically the little trawlers – are getting hammered by measures brought in to govern the larger ones,' said Gary. 'We have genuine quota issues here, horribly confusing legislation and a government policy that seems to be very much steered by the lobbyists and big business. It's a real issue for us. More fishermen are going out of business than I've ever known, and I've been in the industry all my life.'

The fleets of the western Atlantic may have the same problems as the fleets of the eastern Atlantic, but a big difference lies in one of the solutions that has been created. Frustrated by the machinations, contradictions and stonewalling in the legislation governing their industry,

the fishermen had taken charge of their own destiny. These conversations, and these men, were the reason we had come to America – seeking a potential way forward for our own beleaguered fleet.

Inevitably Gary ended up inviting us out on his boat, an offer Nige accepted with alacrity, particularly when he told us that his main source of income was the fabulously abundant lobster populations in the shallow rocky reefs around the inlet.

We met up with Gary a few hours later on the jetty, with Nige virtually hopping from foot to foot with excitement. Gary's boat was a classic Maine lobster vessel, with low gunwales, a wide beam and a large open working area dominated by several water tanks and a winch stooped over the side like some strange metallic heron.

'I wouldn't fancy being out off the Lizard in that,' muttered Nige contemplatively, as the boat manoeuvred alongside. 'Really low freeboard on it. One good blow and you'd be in a world of trouble.' He then did precisely what every person who knows anything about boats will do – lied his head off and complimented Gary warmly on having such a beautiful vessel. Gary beamed and, pleasantries over, we clambered aboard.

'I'm not going far today,' shouted Gary over one shoulder as we motored into the bay. 'I just thought Nige might be interested in how we haul our pots.'

I glanced across at Nige, who was gazing at the landscape as it passed in a series of sculpted inlets and forested coves. He looked entirely content, back in his natural domain with a deck beneath his feet, leaving behind the world of gigantic cars and lady airline pilots.

The water around us was a mass of buoys, hundreds of brightly coloured markers bobbing and twisting in the low chop. We passed a beautiful lighthouse to port.

'That's the lighthouse Forrest Gump runs to in the film,' said Gary, which I shouldn't have found particularly exciting but which for some reason made me very happy indeed. After motoring for a few more minutes, Gary cut back on the throttles and we pulled up alongside the first of his marker buoys.

His boat was only small, lacking the deck space for three people to work alongside one another. I was about to offer Nige the first opportunity to haul a pot while I stood to one side; then I glanced up to see him already in position, gaff in hand. You can take the lobster fisherman out of Cornwall, but you certainly can't remove that all-consuming desire to see what's in the next pot. I silently resolved to stay out of Nige's way during the fishing, lest some serious gaff-related injury resulted.

The winch whined into life and soon the first pot broke the surface. Nige leaned over the side and with an expert flick of the wrist, born and perfected off a rocky headland thousands of miles to the east, he heaved the pot onto the gunwale.

A couple of things struck me straight away. The first was that this pot looked nothing like the ones we used back in Cornwall. The second was that it was absolutely full of lobsters. Those two factors were, strangely enough, closely connected.

The pots used on the eastern seaboard tend to be made of light, brightly coloured wire mesh. Built into one edge is a small gap secured into the side of the pot by rusty metal clips. Gary saw me peering at this and walked over to the pot to turn it towards me.

'This is the escape panel, Monty,' he said, thrusting his fingers through the gap to wiggle them in my direction. 'It's basically

a gap where undersized lobsters can crawl out of the pot. It's hooked in by these clips, which corrode, so if I lose the pot the clips will rust and the whole side panel will fall out. That way we don't have lost pots on the seabed that continue to catch lobster. And see these...' He pointed at a series of plastic tags in the top of the pot. 'These are our annual markers, issued by the Fisheries Authority. It means that they know exactly how many pots are out here fishing and that they can haul a pot at any time, make sure it has one of these tags and so isn't illegal. They can also limit the number of pots in total by issuing only a certain number of tags for that year.'

Having heard many, many complaints about unreasonable legislation over the last six months, this struck me as a very simple, practical solution to monitoring the fishing effort. It was rather nice to hear a fisherman speak of something that actually seemed to work.

Hanging in the middle of the pot, tied in securely by an elaborate knot, was a bait bag. Gary removed this and handed it to Nige to fill from the glittering pile of herring that shifted in the bait box with the movement of the boat.

'It's fairly easy, Nige,' said Gary. 'All you do is fill the bag with bait, tie a knot in the top, then thread the string that's tied to the pot through the bait bag using this tool.' He waved a fearsome-looking spike in our direction. 'You then wrap it round this clip in the top of the pot. Simple.'

But it wasn't simple. A fact that would drive Nige practically insane over the next couple of hours.

It was fascinating to see how the different systems for putting bait in a pot had evolved over the years on opposite sides of the Atlantic. This isn't to say that the Cornish way of doing things is always

better, it's just different. The snag here is that – when it comes to putting bait in a bag in a lobster pot – our way *is* better. By a mile. This placed Nige in a dilemma because as a guest on someone else's boat and a very nice chap indeed, there's no way he would have dreamed of mentioning it.

Off Cornwall, as a pot is opened, a drawstring attached to the lid slackens off and the mouth of the bait bag loosens. Bait is then stuffed into the bag while it's still attached to the pot, the lid is closed (thus tightening the string around the neck of the bag) and the pot is duly chucked over the side. A rather elegant solution to the problem of putting fish in a net bag and keeping it there, even if I do say so myself.

'The fishery has been – and remains – a huge success, with record catches year upon year'

As the afternoon progressed, I could see Nige working himself into an indignant froth as each pot that came up had the bag removed by hand, was duly carried to the bait box, filled with herring, brought back to the pot and then tied in using a knot that would have made any ancient mariner proud. This took perhaps a minute at the most, but the technique back in Cornwall took about 15 seconds. Just think of all those lost seconds over the years. I considered it an interesting variation in technique, whereas Nige became positively incandescent about it. There are a great many things the Americans do better than us – industry, technological development, military might – but when it comes to stuffing putrefying fish into a lobster pot

and keeping it there, we beat them hands down. And for Nige, when he considered the parallel cultural development of our two great nations, this was clearly a top priority.

A further interesting development was Gary removing a real bruiser of a lobster from one of the pots, its shell a gorgeous dark claret. The American lobster is a different species to the European one, with one of its defining characteristics being the red of its carapace, as opposed to ours, which have a blue shell. As anyone who has eaten a fresh lobster will know, European lobster go red only when they are cooked, which to my eyes made every single American lobster we caught look instantly and absolutely delicious.

Gary regarded the monster lobster briefly, turning it weightily in one hand, before lobbing it back over the side without even measuring it. This provoked a stunned silence from the British contingent on board.

Gary laughed. 'We have an upper size limit here too,' he explained, reaching into the wheelhouse and waggling the measure in our direction. 'The idea is that when a lobster gets to a certain size, it should be left on the seabed to breed. It seems to work, you know. We're in better shape as a fishery than we have been for years.'

And work it unequivocally does. There are about 7,000 lobster fishermen along the coast of Maine, each working up to 800 pots. This is along a coastline of only 3,500 miles, so we're talking about two fishermen for every mile, or 1,600 pots if you're looking at it from a lobster's point of view. This is also very much a shallow, inshore fishery, so the pressure on every reef and rocky outcrop is intense. And yet the simple measures of monitoring the number of pots, allowing undersize lobsters to scuttle out of the escape panel and returning all lobsters over a certain size, have reaped tremendous rewards.

The Maine lobster fishery is now one of the most successful on earth and is a fine example of local expertise being combined with sound management legislation. Since 1947 the catches have been stable and since 1948 the fishermen have been V-notching females carrying eggs – a similar system to that applied by the inshore fishermen in the UK. But it is the management of the fishery as a whole that presents a particularly heart-warming story.

In 1995 the Maine Legislature enacted what they termed a 'co-management policy'. This divided the coastline into seven zones and turned over control of those zones to elected committees of local fishermen. Defying expectations, the fishermen duly introduced legislation limiting the number of total pots used per boat, strictly controlling the licences issued and even monitoring the time of day fishing could take place. The result was directly in front of me in the bustling, clicking mass of lobsters that sat in the holding tank on board the boat. The fishery has been – and remains – a huge success, with record catches year upon year.

Soon the sun began to set and Gary turned the boat back home. It had been a fascinating glimpse of another fishery, a parallel world of rocky shores and cold Atlantic currents, yet with subtle variations that had worked wonders for a stressed environment. As we stepped ashore in Port Clyde, securing the ropes to the weathered pilings as we did so, Gary shouted up to us for one last time from the boat.

'So, guys, what do you think of Maine lobster fishing?'

Nige glanced down, looking first at the boat, then the tank full of lobsters and finally a lone bait bag that had come free from a pot. His brow furrowed, he took half a pace towards the edge of the quay, opened his mouth to speak and then settled back on his heels with a sigh.

'It's been bloody marvellous, Gary,' he said, smiling and lifting one hand in a brief salute.

Some things, it seems, are best kept in Cornwall.

* * *

As is the way with fishing communities the world over, the hospitality Gary had shown us on board the boat extended onto dry land as well. He kindly invited us to a local restaurant for dinner, which was very good news indeed as it gave us a chance to meet his wife Kim.

Some people are a force of nature, an unstoppable elemental power that carries all before it. Kim had blazed a trail in changing the way fish is marketed and perceived in Maine, creating a system that was now sweeping the entire country. I looked forward to meeting her very much and wasn't disappointed when she bustled into the foyer.

She was short, loud, very friendly and talked a great deal. She had that characteristic American approach to strangers, looking them straight in the eye and treating them with respect, interest and familiarity. As a tightly wrapped Englishman, constrained by years of protocol and reserve, I blushed and stammered as I was enveloped in a hug of considerable fragrance and dimensions. Nige, on the other hand, thought it was great and beamed as she trilled, 'Nigel Legge – I've heard *so* much about you', before embracing him warmly.

Over dinner, Kim explained a little – well, quite a lot actually – about the project that

she, Gary and her brother-in-law Glenn had established. It was called a Community Supported Fishery or CSF.

'It just seemed so ridiculous,' she said, between mouthfuls of a phenomenally badly cooked fish. I glanced down at my own grey, gently steaming mound of unidentifiable chowder. Why do so many American restaurants feel the need to smother everything in cheese, I wondered briefly. To take a beautiful fresh wild fish, flesh delicate and flaking, the very essence of the sea, to boil it until it virtually disintegrates, and then to smother it in two pounds of cheddar seems a bit strange to me.

Snapping out of my reverie, I looked up again at Kim, who was in full flow.

'There was Gary, heading out and taking all the risks to catch the fish, and yet we had no control whatsoever over what price it made as it went to the large markets for auction. It was also being distributed all over the country and lost so much of its freshness, ending up as this nondescript product in a plastic pack hundreds of miles away from where it was caught.'

This problem is certainly not unique to the United States. The Western world in general has strayed a very long way from the original sustainable model of relying on fresh produce from local fishing ports. Fish that masquerades as 'fresh' in a UK supermarket is frequently anything but, and we're not talking a few days old either. Incidentally, if you happen to be eating a fish supper at this precise moment, you might like to delicately push your meal to one side before reading on.

The vast majority of fish we eat today goes through four simple stages. In the first it is caught and gutted. In the second it undergoes primary processing, which mainly involves being filleted. This takes place either at sea in large processing vessels, or in shore-based facilities. In recent years these facilities have tended to be in places such as Eastern Europe or the Far East, due to the presence of cheap labour. The third stage is called secondary processing, which is where the fish may be de-boned, breaded, cooked and then packaged. The final stage is export to a grateful consumer, who may well live very close to where the fish was originally caught but will be eating a product with more air miles than Alan Whicker.

The real delays occur between stages three and four – the final processing and the delivery to the consumer. Between these stages the fish is stored. International trading in fish takes place in units called 'blocks' – a neat term for a 7.5-kilogram lump of frozen fish, which may consist of fillets, flesh or indeed entire fish. A block may have several owners during the course of numerous trades and can be stored for anything from three to five months. In a recent particularly notorious case, food officials found a warehouse in Lincolnshire with blocks that were five years old.

Inevitably with a supply chain that snakes around the world, the original source of the fish we eat becomes somewhat lost in the ether. How about some lovely Pacific cod, anyone? They're more sustainable than their heavily fished Atlantic counterparts, as labelled and neatly laid out on a fish counter in one of the major British supermarkets. The snag is that 20 per cent of them are actually Atlantic cod; it's just that somewhere in the immense supply chain things got a little mixed up. Scampi? Always a winner, but not when you learn that it contains only 18 per cent scampi and that the rest is made up of a mash of heaven only knows what else. Good old fish and chips? You can't go wrong with that, surely? Well, only if when you're ordering you say, 'I'd like some battered pangasius please – or Vietnamese river cobbler, as you might call it. Salt and vinegar – ooh yes, in fact, now I come to think of it, make that soy sauce.' A certain chippie in Worcestershire was prosecuted for flogging this when they said it was cod, but you can only begin to imagine what lies beneath the batter elsewhere.

Once the demand for fish is deemed sufficient, the blocks in the holding facilities are released and turned into what we ultimately purchase – a fillet that may be several months old, frequently sourced from overseas, processed overseas and then sold in a packet with a picture of a brightly painted fishing boat on the wrapper.

In 2007 the UK imported 672,000 tonnes of fish, worth £1.76 billion. In the same period our fleet caught 366,000 tonnes of fish, worth £368 million. This means that almost two-thirds of what we eat is not caught by our fishermen.

This is particularly odd as we live on an island in the cold, rich waters of the North Atlantic, with one of the longest traditions of fishing of any nation on earth. And yet as we sit down to dinner we eat cod and haddock from Iceland. We tuck into salmon from Norway and America. We make salads out of cold-water prawns from Denmark, as well as tuna from Mauritius and the Seychelles. For a little treat we spoil ourselves with warm-water prawns from Thailand, India and Bangladesh. As we do so our own small-boat fishermen are dumping 40 to 50 per cent of the fish they catch overboard due to quota restrictions and are quietly going out of business.

In the USA the problem is even more extreme, with a whopping 85 per cent of all fish eaten being imported from overseas.

Gary, his brother Glenn and Kim herself spotted the profound flaws in this system. The mass market, and the huge distribution costs of wholesalers, meant that the fishermen were getting a price for their fish that barely covered the cost of their fuel. The Port Clyde fishermen's catch varied throughout the year – much the same as every shore-based fishery anywhere in the world – with cod, haddock and hake caught in the summer, and shrimp and lobster in the winter. They simply had to seek out a means of getting slightly more money or the entire fleet would fail, causing the demise of a 300-year-old fishing community.

'We decided,' said Gary, as he attacked the plate of food in front of him, 'that actually catching less fish of better quality would be better for everyone. Less fish means a better price locally, but for that you need to provide a really good-quality product. We also decided that transport of that fish should be kept to an absolute minimum. We worked with the Gulf of Maine Research Institute who developed gear for us that fished much more sustainably. Our by-catch dropped off and we realised we were onto something.'

'We decided to go straight to our potential customers,' chimed in Kim. 'Through a wholesaler we were getting 50 cents a pound for fish and yet we knew our friends in the community would happily pay more than that to get fresh fish, sustainably caught, to keep their local fishing fleet in business.'

And so, tentatively, with many an administrative glitch and table-thumping argument, America's first Community Supported Fishery emerged. The idea was – as with all truly magnificent ideas – breathtakingly simple.

'Basically, the customer pays a lump sum up-front at the start of the fishing season.

They then pick up fresh fish once a week for the next three months,' said Kim. 'It's an injection of cash for the fishermen when they need it most – at the start of the new fishing year.'

'We started with a local church group,' piped up Gary, 'but very quickly we had 200 local people banging on the door to become involved. They each paid $300 and with so many customers involved it meant $60,000 or so could be distributed between the boats taking part in the scheme.'

'In simple terms, it means that the average price of the fish they provided for the CSF went from 50 cents a pound to $3 a pound,' said Kim, with considerable pride. 'It kept several of them in business, you know, a real lifeline. But is also meant that once a week we had local people turning up, at a local venue, to collect locally caught fish that was so fresh you might as well snorkel for it yourself. And their money went straight to their local small-boat fleet, which was fishing far more sustainably than the larger vessels.'

'The only way you can get fresher fish is by being a gannet,' said Gary, laying down his knife and fork with a triumphant clatter. 'In short, everyone wins.' He wiped the corner of his mouth with a napkin and sat back with a smile. Which was fair enough. If ever a chap deserved to look proud of himself, I thought, it was probably Gary.

Such was the success of the CSF in Port Clyde that it led to a local funding body becoming involved in order to develop the system further. The money from the Island Institute resulted in the creation of a small processing facility just outside the port, which Kim suggested we look round the next day.

* * *

Just as dawn was breaking the next morning we duly drove up in our vast black limousine and, feeling rather like extras from an episode of *The Sopranos*, self-consciously climbed out in the car park next to a large and ugly white hangar. Gary was out fishing and so had arranged for his brother Glenn – chairman of the Fishermen's Association and something of a driving force behind the CSF – to meet us at the facility.

Glenn was a large man who plainly didn't do small talk. He was perfectly pleasant, he just didn't feel the need to smile, make chitchat or ask fatuous questions. This always turns me into a gibbering idiot.

'Well, Glenn, hello, ah ha ha, how nice to ... ermmm ... blimey, nice facility,' I babbled as I walked across the car park with him and the silence lengthened.

Glenn and Nige glanced across at me as if I were an idiot, which I suspect – at that moment – was a fair assumption. I could hardly wait to get into the processing building so there would be something to look at other than Glenn's stony visage.

The plant sat next to a perfect little harbour – a classic Port Clyde scene with an absurdly picturesque cove bordered by weathered wooden pilings. The building looked fairly dilapidated, but lights glowed in the windows even at this early hour and plainly there was much going on within. Glenn wordlessly held open the front door and waved Nige and me into the warmth of the front office.

The tour proved very interesting indeed, with the three staff inside fastidiously picking the flesh out of crabs or filleting fish. This was all done with real precision, with one girl even working on a lightboard that wouldn't have looked out of place during open-heart surgery. I asked her what she was doing.

'Picking out parasitic worms,' she said cheerily, waving one in my direction. 'All fresh fish have them, although our customers don't seem to appreciate that as a sign of freshness too much.' She laughed and bent back to her work.

Everywhere there was an air of endeavour and civic pride, with the final stage being Glenn opening a large freezer and showing me – straight-faced – a neatly vacuum-packed fillet of fish.

'We freeze some of it,' he said, 'but as much as possible we get out to the consumer absolutely fresh. It's the way fish should be eaten.'

I agreed enthusiastically, as did Nige. This was an inspiring operation, a place where the fishermen of a small community had entirely taken charge of their own destiny. After many months of singularly bleak conversations back in the UK about the future of the fishing fleet, it was positively uplifting to see a scheme characterised by such drive and initiative.

I said as much to Glenn as we left and thought I saw a twitch at one corner of his mouth, which may or may not have been the passing shadow of a proud smile. Then again it might just have been the wind. Or wind.

'Thanks, Monty,' he said. 'We're not out of the woods yet financially, but we're getting there.'

He shook our hands and we left him standing in the car park. The last I saw of him was in the rear-view mirror, one hand raised in a laconic farewell, looking slightly glum with the magnificent achievement of the processing plant framed behind him.

* * *

It would have been positively criminal to come to this part of the world and not visit Gloucester. This was one of many towns on the eastern seaboard of the United States that was named by homesick settlers as they looked wistfully east. As I peered at the road map I could see Dartmouth, Plymouth, Dorchester, Belfast and Bangor, to name but a few. Mixed in with these were Native American and French names, the violent history of this coastline writ large in every road sign and village name board along the highway.

Gloucester was settled in 1623. Life for the early pioneers was certainly not an endless series of turkey shoots, barn building and vigorous infection of the locals. It was in fact brutally harsh and after a short, lethal stay the colony was abandoned in 1626. It was gradually resettled over the next few years and officially named in 1642. The original boundaries included the town of Rockport nearby, but after a falling out about religion in 1840 Gloucester went it alone. And they've been doing things pretty much their own way ever since.

It is fishing that has always defined this town and continues to do so to this day. But the fishing undertaken by the men of Gloucester has always been of a particularly unforgiving nature. The vast numbers of cod discovered offshore were there because of a geological quirk – two great banks that rose from deep water. Here the currents converged and upwellings created an abundance of food. Where the cod gathered, so did the fishermen, their hunting grounds the mighty oceanic mountains beneath their keels. The first was Georges Bank, a mere 150-mile voyage offshore; the second the Grand Banks, a thousand miles out from Gloucester – northeast into an unforgiving ocean. This was the type of fishing where fortunes were made, the type of fishing to make men crazy with the

'Gloucester has the air of a town on the edge, peering towards an uncertain horizon' intoxicating whiff of profit and the type of fishing that reaped a terrible harvest in lost ships and men.

Having driven the hour or so from Port Clyde, Nige and I stood on the shore at Gloucester and looked up at one of the most famous fishing monuments on earth.

It is known simply as 'The Man at the Wheel' and depicts a figure braced on deck, gripping an old-style ship's wheel with straight arms, chin lifted and eyes staring into the storm ahead. It is a fine monument, a fitting tribute to the defiance and devilry required to venture out onto the heaving wilderness of the banks. Lower your eyes from the monument and the price of that defiance is inscribed at your feet: vast ranks of names, etched in brass and glinting in the morning sun. It is the very identity of Gloucester, carved by those who were left behind. Not for nothing did one historian note that the history of this town has been written in tears.

Between 1860 and 1906, there were 660 ships lost from Gloucester, a community that even today numbers only 30,000 inhabitants. During that same period, 3,880 men were lost. Since records began, an estimated 10,000 men have been killed, with one storm alone in 1862 claiming 15 schooners and 120 fishermen. Such was the carnage that a local skipper – Captain Joseph Collins – was moved to cry, 'When will the slaughter cease?' as yet another boat failed to return.

The most famous loss in recent times has been *Andrea Gail*, the swordfishing boat depicted in the film *The Perfect Storm*. By a pure coincidence we arrived on the 20th anniversary to the day of the boat's disappearance, a fact made all the more stark as we were staying in the Crow's Nest, the bar where the men who were lost drank their final beer.

The immense endeavour and sacrifice of the most sustained fishing effort in history soon saw the Banks stripped of their fish. The demise of cod in the North Atlantic has been well documented and the result has seen Gloucester become a pale ghost of the great fishing port of memory. In 1890 there were nearly 400 schooners based in the harbour; now only a shadow of these great fleets remain. The descendants of the Sicilian, Portuguese and Irish fishermen who emigrated to take part in this maritime gold rush are now watching their own boats go out of business. Gloucester has the air of a town on the edge, peering towards an uncertain horizon as the very essence of the community slips from view.

As one of the responses to its fishing crisis, Gloucester has developed a particularly successful Community Supported Fishery. I was keen for Nigel and me to find out a little more about it before we returned home. Our timing, though, posed a slight problem. Here we were in a blue-collar town that was experiencing times of unprecedented hardship, having turned up bang on the anniversary of the loss of their most famous vessel. It didn't seem to me to be the ideal moment to wander into a bar and start asking questions. Nige, though, was completely unfazed.

'Ah, it'll be fine, Mont,' he said as we unloaded our monstrous car outside the Crow's Nest later that morning. 'Fishermen are the same everywhere. You mark my words, I'll wander over to the scariest-looking bloke in there and we'll be chatting away before you know it.'

I wondered briefly what I would do should Nige get chinned. He was my mentor, my friend and had become almost a father figure to me. And yet as he vanished under a flashing array of expertly

THEY THAT GO
DOWN TO THE SEA
IN SHIPS
1623 — 1923

wielded filleting knives and vigorously pumping right arms, would I leap in to defend him? I liked to think I would, but then again the car was very close to the front door, was massive, stoutly constructed and had excellent central locking. I decided that I'd wait and see.

We pushed open the door of the bar and stepped into the dimly lit interior. I wouldn't say that the jukebox fell silent and the pool balls stopped rolling, but there was a distinct 'moment' as we entered. I wasn't as strong as Nige, but I was definitely quicker off the mark, so I surreptitiously positioned myself for a clear run at the exit.

The interior looked precisely as you'd imagine it should. There was a large central square bar, at which sat several people who were unmistakably fishermen. Sizeable moustaches were in abundance, as were dirty baseball hats pushed back from the weathered features beneath. Around the walls were fading photos and tattered images of boats lost and men vanished. A flickering neon sign illuminated the far recesses of the room, highlighting two very drunk men as they slumped at a table in a scene straight out of a B-movie.

Nige dropped his bag and strode straight up to the nearest figure at the bar, a substantial bearded man with a beer bottle gripped in one meaty paw. 'Roight on, roight on,' he said with a smile, extending his hand, 'my name's Nige and I'm from the Lizard in Cornwall. I catch lobster.'

The beard twitched slightly, a mystified expression flitted across the small amount of features that were visible and the hand not holding the beer bottle extended to grip Nige's.

'Hi there. Joe's the name.' His accent was a glorious amalgamation of Irish and Italian, history resonating in every word. 'I catch lobster, too. Welcome to Gloucester.'

Fast-forward several hours and we were sitting at a table in the corner, its top now hidden by a clinking array of beer bottles. Our bags sat where they had been dropped by the door, forgotten as the conversation rolled and surged around us. It had been a splendid afternoon.

Joe had introduced us to one of the greatest men it has ever been my pleasure to meet. His name was Jack and his opening riposte will take some beating in any conversation I expect to have for the remainder of my days.

'Hi,' he said quietly, 'I'm Jack. Fishing out of Gloucester right now, but I've been harpooning swordfish most of my life. I've chased them all the way from Newfoundland to Venezuela.'

Nige and I were struck somewhat dumb by this: suddenly taking lobsters out of pots off the Lizard wasn't quite so impressive.

'Blimey,' I said eventually, 'what's that like?'

'Well,' said Jack thoughtfully, 'a fully grown swordfish weighs about the same as a Harley-Davidson. More, probably. Imagine a Harley thundering past you on a highway and you hook a line on it, then try to slow it down. Well, it's like that.'

'Blimey,' I said again, although this time rather more quietly.

Jack was a truly extraordinary man. Now in his mid-60s, he was a Vietnam veteran who had led a *Boy's Own* life packed with adventure. He told us of creeping up on the vast shadows of resting swordfish, harpoon aloft, arm cocked, rope coiled and blood thundering.

'It's their poop,' he said, rather mysteriously, 'that's how you find them. They leave a slick on the surface when they go to the toilet. It glints in the sun and you home in on it. Then the battle begins.' He cackled and took a sip of his beer, eyes alive at the memory.

'Is that why they call it a poop deck?' I said wittily. Nige and Jack glanced across at me and then returned immediately to their conversation.

Jack talked of great tropical storms, of men lost and of a lifetime of tiptoeing along the meniscus of the ocean, following the blue curve of the earth in the wake of mighty fish.

'I'm the last of them, I expect,' he said. 'It's a dying business. I'm not a militant by any means, but there comes a point when you must do something. I understand the need for conservation, I really do, but we must all work together on this. Here in America it's big business that holds sway and the little man with the small boat is being killed off. It's no good for anyone or anything – not the fish, not the fleet and certainly not the community.'

Jack told us of three mighty Irish vessels that had arrived in Gloucester only a few years before. Unable to fish effectively in European waters due to their colossal capacity, they had simply relocated across the Atlantic. He waved a beer glass in the direction of the harbour.

'You can see them. Look, over there alongside.'

And sure enough there they were on the far side of the dock, lights burning in the late afternoon. Three colossal vessels – like tower blocks toppled onto their sides.

'I don't know,' said Jack. 'What's better for a community like this? One vessel like that catching a thousand tons of fish in a week, or a thousand smaller boats catching a ton each? I think the answer is fairly obvious, don't you?'

Finally, after a clinking salute to the men lost on *Andrea Gail* 20 years before, the last beer was sunk. It was time to head off for a few hours' sleep.

* * *

The next morning was, as ever in the world of fishing, an early start. We had been invited out on a trawler called *Razzo* to work the fishing grounds directly outside Gloucester. It was to be a short trip, probably only four hours in duration; the idea was for Nige and me to follow the fish we caught through to the Community Supported Fishery customers, who would collect their share later that same day.

We deployed the trawl in the soft light of dawn and then rumbled in companionable silence for several hours as the sun rose on the bow. Having hauled the nets and filled several fish boxes with cod, haddock and pollack, we turned smartly on our broad heel and were back in Gloucester tucking into a doughnut and coffee by 8 a.m. It was almost civilised.

It was the final stage that I really wanted to see. Even as we sat in the coffee shop, the fish was undergoing its primary processing – essentially a simple filleting operation. As office workers bustled past us to grab their morning cappuccino, wrinkling their noses at the ripe odour of the two slimy fishermen in their midst, I could actually see the small processing house through the steamed-up windows of the cafe. The fish that had been sculling through dark canyons only hours before, bathed in icy North Atlantic water, were nearing the last phase of their journey.

We were due to meet up with Steve Parkes and Heather Fraelick from the Community Supported Fishery later that morning. After lunch, which was doughnuts followed by some more doughnuts, we duly turned up at yet another beautiful clapperboard building

just back from the seafront. A sign swung in the light sea breeze: 'Turner's Seafood Market and Fish Fry – Anything Fresher Still Swims!' This was the operating base for the CSF.

Steve was hairy. Very hairy indeed. As he shook my hand, it struck me that he was the absolute perfect front for an organisation that represented small-boat fishermen so nobly. He looked very much as if he had just rounded a storm-lashed cape while strapped to a wildly spinning ship's wheel, before retiring to his hammock below to chew briefly on a bit of bull kelp. If there was anyone who should be handing out fresh Atlantic fish, it was Steve.

Heather had recently been taken on as a PR expert for the Gloucester CSF. She told me of the relationship they had already established with city workers in nearby Boston.

'It's been the most fantastic thing to witness,' she said. 'We've now got lots of very committed people in the city who turn up once a week to pick up their fish. They know they're supporting the small boats when they do it, they know it's sustainably caught and they know it's the freshest fish it's possible to eat.' She paused for a moment as Steve passed behind her, a large cool box held between bristly fists. 'We're all quite evangelical about it, really.' She laughed and looked slightly embarrassed at her own enthusiasm.

The distribution point was at a large garden centre on the outskirts of Boston itself. By the time we arrived it was early evening. It was also Halloween – a festival embraced with genuine fervour in the US – and there were giant pumpkins as far as the eye could see. Nige and I parked up in the gathering gloom, wove our way through the immense, multicoloured

aisles and found Steve being very hairy at the back of the shop. He had placed the cool box next to a large counter, a neatly typed list on its lid. He gave us a friendly wave as we approached.

Over the next two hours a steady stream of well-dressed – and, as it was Halloween, some rather bizarrely dressed – city workers filed through the garden centre to pick up their fish. I chatted briefly to one lady, somewhat unnerved by the fact that she was dressed as a ghoul and had two tiny goblins accompanying her. As I spoke one of them snarled at me and waved a plastic skull, which I must confess put me off the exchange a tad.

'Oh, it's wonderful,' said the ghoul, waving her bag of cod. 'To know that we're supporting the small boats is good enough, but every week we're told what fish to expect and even given little recipe cards when we pick them up. We've also had gutting and filleting demonstrations from the fishermen – it was so nice to actually meet them and talk about their work.'

'Our dinner has eyes,' said one of the goblins, a voice piping up from knee height.

'Oh, there's that as well,' said the ghoul with a smile. 'The kids love to see the fish – they're like exotic monsters from another galaxy. Anyway, must get on.'

She bustled off, bringing to an end one of the more surreal conversations of my life. The goblins skipped on either side of her, trying very hard to look into the plastic bag she was carrying: bizarre creatures from one world peering intently at strange beings from another.

CHAPTER **8** **FAREWELL TO CADGWITH**

December announced its arrival with a thunderclap, an explosion of sound and fury launched from the very heart of the Atlantic.

Walking down to the cove one particularly wild morning I had to lean into the wind, buffeted by each blast. The horizon was black with immense clouds, heavy with rain and full of dark intent. This was the first proper storm I had witnessed and, as there was absolutely no chance of the fleet heading out to sea, I decided to walk up the coast path to the high point of the Huer's Hut, perched on the headland overlooking the village and the beach.

Puffing and panting, I stepped from the relative protection of the hedges lining the path and onto the exposed headland. The wind shrieked and howled around me, tugging at my clothing as I inched towards the cliff edge. I looked down into the cove and saw only a mass of foam, the rock walls amplifying the roar of the waves as they thumped and hissed onto the shingle. The boats had been drawn up high onto the road and for the first time they looked inconsequential to me, hollow wooden shells that men in their innocence believed would protect them from the forces the ocean could unleash.

I lifted my eyes to the horizon and saw the Lizard enveloped in colossal towers of spray, hundreds of thousands of tons of energy dissipating every second as the waves crashed headlong into the cliffs. It seemed to me that nothing could withstand such a relentless, implacable force and that surely the headland must crumble under the fury of the assault. With every impact I felt the ground tremble beneath my feet, as though each swell was a mortal blow. After a few minutes crouched in the lee of the hut, I decided that enough was enough and turned on my heel to scurry back down the path to the sanctuary of Nige's shed.

Nige was already in residence, his signature mug of coffee steaming on the windowsill, creating a mini fog bank that climbed the pitted glass. Winter was Nige's main time for making withy pots; the shed was strewn with slender sticks of willow while the skeleton of a pot sat on the stand, half finished as Nige peered at it from across the room.

'Ah, Mont,' he said as I entered, stamping my feet and blowing out my cheeks, 'nice to see you. Kettle's just boiled – make yourself a brew and grab a seat. I'm just working on this pot, so we can chat as I go along if you like. I would ask you to help, but you're crap at it if my memory serves me correctly.'

This was an entirely valid point, besides which I was very happy to sit close to the heater, hot drink in hand, and do nothing more than natter. As the wind rattled the corrugated iron of the roof and shook the old door on its hinges, it seemed an entirely appropriate way to see off what was left of the morning.

'Bit poor, isn't it, Mont?' Nige said as he eyed the pot, twisting a sharpened withy spar in his hand.

'It's horrendous, Nige. So much nicer to be sitting in here wishing we were out fishing than to be out fishing wishing we were in here.'

He smiled. 'Good point. Mind you, nowadays there's really no excuse for getting caught out in a storm if you're a day boat. The technology for predicting

weather is so good, and the information so easily available, that you've only yourself to blame if you get it wrong.'

He grunted as he spotted the right slot for the withy and vigorously worked it into the pot, twisting and weaving it into place before bending down to pick up another.

'In the old days the only way they could predict storms were little bits of intuition and folklore. Do you know what a sand hopper is?'

I did indeed. Any pile of rotting seaweed would be infested with them, tiny flea-like amphipods that leapt and flicked in swarms when exposed to the air.

'Well, the way the old men knew a storm was coming was that the sand hoppers would all move up the beach and actually infest the houses along the road. They'd detect the low-pressure systems, you see, and know they had to move away from the waves. It's a long way from the internet, isn't it?'

He paused once again before thrusting the latest stick into the pot.

'Mind you,' he went on, talking as he worked, 'there were plenty that got it wrong. Winter is a very difficult time if you're a fisherman. The weather is generally pretty bad, money is always tight and the combination of those two things sometimes made you go out when you shouldn't. Even today I worry about the younger skippers pushing things a bit too hard.'

His words hung in the air between us. The financial pressure on the men who skipper the small boats of Cadgwith has always been intense and, as the storms gathered and the nights lengthened, the situation could become almost unbearable. It seemed as good a moment as ever to broach the subject of the Community Supported Fishery we'd witnessed over in America.

'Well, Mont,' said Nige later, taking a seat in the threadbare armchair next to the fire, having temporarily abandoned the pot-building, 'it's a nice concept, don't get me wrong. I just don't know if it would work here.' He looked down at his hands as he spoke, the tools of his trade. There was a hint of regret in his voice as he continued. 'I'm not sure people are that interested in the fishing fleets any more, to be honest.'

Nige was right about most things relating to fishing and the sea, and I had learned some time ago that it was sensible to defer to him in all matters nautical. But in this case I genuinely believed he was wrong.

* * *

On the face of it this is indeed one of those small tragedies, a manifestation of modern life. Over the course of the last century, swept along in the relentless march of industrialisation, we have somehow lost that intimate connection with our maritime heritage. The fact is that we as a nation don't understand our fishing fleet any more – but that's not to say we are not fascinated by them.

In the course of my previous work as a marine biologist, I had seen the alchemy of awakening that connection we all have with the sea. I had witnessed classes of inner-city children come alive when I showed them images of great fish in distant oceans. As I sat in Nige's shed, mug in hand and the detritus of withy pots scattered before me, I quietly resolved that, in the few weeks that remained of my time in Cadgwith, I would show him and his fellow skippers that there was still a fascination and affection for their kind. With this there might come a glimmer of hope, a chance to build on the last remnants of the connection between British fishing folk and the island they once supplied.

As it was early December the country was just cranking into gear for the festival of unfettered commercialism that is a modern Christmas. I love Christmas and throw genuine tantrums unless certain precise rituals are followed in our household on the big day. These include the Queen's Speech, eating to the point of internal injury and the understated, smouldering resentment that is the British signature of any family gathering. But this year the festive season also represented something of an opportunity.

'I wanted every child attending the turning-on of the Christmas lights to go home reeking of fish slime'

The run-up to Christmas was heralded by a number of events in Helston, the local market town. The first of these was due to take place within a week – the grand switching-on of the Christmas lights. For this Helston would turn out in all its Yuletide finery. There would be toffee apples, market stalls, fairground rides, mulled wine and several fights. Everyone would then trail home happy that tradition had been honoured. What the occasion gave me was people, lots of whom I was convinced would know very little about fishing, all gathered together in a confined space and looking for something to do.

Having bid Nige farewell in the shed, I walked back to the Old Cellars with the brisk stride of a man with a plan. I would set up a stall with Nige and Jonathan Fletcher – the latter a Porthleven fisherman who ran a part-time fish shop in Cadgwith. He was a great advocate of introducing the

wider population to the joys of British seafood and in the summer I had often seen him standing in the entrance of the shop, waving monkfish at alarmed tourists and enthusing about anatomy and texture. Jonathan was a particularly eloquent character, thin as a crane, a walking collection of right angles and pithy one-liners. I knew he would relish the chance to chat to all and sundry about various piscine wonders, and sure enough one phone call swiftly engaged his services.

Our plan was to create a stall where nothing was for sale, but everything was there to be touched, to be handled and to be studied. Roll up, roll up and gawk. I wanted every child attending the turning-on of the Christmas lights to go home reeking of fish slime, with their parents babbling away about the life history of the ballan wrasse (which, let me tell you, is pretty damn exciting). We would offer a crab-picking demonstration, a 'Guess the Weight of the Crab' stand and a 'Guess the Fish Species' counter. The fishermen would also, crucially, encourage the parents to sign up to take part in the first ever Community Supported Fishery scheme in the country.

With this in mind, the whole of the next week was spent pretty much exclusively on the scrounge. Tables, table cloths, fish tubs, interesting spiky specimens from the boats' daily catches, fairy lights and even a large sign that Nige created just to get me to shut up about the large sign I wanted him to create. The great day dawned, and soon the three of us were loading up Nige's little white van and rattling our way into Helston.

Nige muttered under his breath as we set up shop, not convinced that anyone would show the slightest interest. He was right to be mildly concerned in that we were

somewhat off the main street, but even so a steady stream of curious onlookers filed past as we self-consciously erected the trestle table and hung our massive 'Cadgwith Fresh Catch' banner over the top of it.

Nige and Jonathan laid out their bowls and crab-picking tools, like surgeons in oilskins. A group of teenagers wandered past, drunk on surging hormones and cheap cider, pausing only to sneer and shout at the scene before them. I smiled to myself as they did so, knowing that the two 60-year-old fishermen they were taunting could bend them into more interesting shapes than your average balloon animal if they chose to do so. If you see a man – or men – in oilskins, be nice. It'll keep you in the gene pool longer. Nige and Jonathan simply carried on laying out the stall, not even glancing up at the group who swiftly lost interest and stumbled off down the street.

'In the box was history, piracy, death, conflict and heroism'

I looked down at the box at my feet and knew that within it was genuine magic. The contents would awaken something primal in the passers-by, igniting a dormant strand of DNA to bring them alive. In the box, shining and sleek, I had fish.

But not just fish. In the box was history, piracy, death, conflict and heroism. In the box was the story of our fishing fleets. I had a cod, a dappled aristocrat over whom wars had been fought, tens of thousands of lives had been lost and from whom millions of eggs could pour forth in a single year. I had

a red mullet, a gleaming ruby of a fish, so valuable that in Roman times the only way to pay for one was with the equivalent weight in silver. I had a wrasse, a gaudy speckled beast over 20 years old with teeth in its throat and a reproductive strategy that sees it change from female to male in its own lifetime. I had a red gurnard, a sea robin with legs that strode the seabed in glistening red armour. I had a John Dory, a pewter sliver with a mouth that could extend miraculously to a third of the length of its entire body. Two dark marks on its flanks were said to be the finger- and thumbprint of St Peter as he had lifted the fish out of the water, so here was an animal that appeared by religious appointment. And I had a dogfish, a small shark equipped with the battery of senses that made it just as much of a sinuous hunter as any great white.

Every muscular back, curved tooth and delicate fin spoke of another world. This was a dark, echoing, mysterious place of monsters and mystery, and I knew that once the box was opened we would be mobbed.

By the time we had finished setting up, the tepid winter sun had slipped beneath the horizon, giving way to a Cornish dusk that bled the light and heat from the day.

The lights were switched on, a moment heralded for us by a small Christmas tree suspended overhead flickering into life and a ragged cheer coming from the main street in the near distance. Soon the crowds began to trickle back from around the corner and as they neared, like some conjuror of old, I whipped the cover from the fish box with a theatrical flourish.

The result was instantaneous and deliciously predictable. Immediately small children in the crowd wormed their way free from their parents' hands and ran towards the fish as they gleamed eerily in the multicoloured lights. Even as the cover settled on the street, the first small fingers were stroking the back of the dogfish, frowning at the rasp of fingertip on the tiny denticles of the skin. I lifted up a giant crab and the children ran shrieking from range, the braver ones gradually edging closer once the initial shock had faded. This was a great armoured monster, a Hollywood special effect brought to life. I glanced across at Nige and Jonathan, both of whom were furiously dishing out white, delicate crab meat to appreciative parents. Nige glanced back and slowly shook his head with a half smile.

The next couple of hours were bedlam. There was one incident with a drunk man and a spider crab that could have gone very wrong indeed, but was fortunately averted by Jonathan's swift intervention. Someone tried to run off with the wrasse, but was detained due to their being only four years old and not entirely in control of their legs. Even the crowd of teenagers returned and proudly photographed each other as they gingerly held up cod and conger.

But the real aim of the evening was to get people to embrace the idea of the CSF. This was a fishing expedition of a different kind, an attempt to garner a list of names from the assembled masses. Goaded on by their kids, and perhaps desperate to get their offspring away from this smelly corner of a side street, more and more of the parents signed up to the concept. This was despite the fact that the vast majority had no idea what the concept actually was, as explanations were getting somewhat blurred in the feeding frenzy of excited children wrestling over increasingly ragged-looking fish. By the time we had finished, we had a scrawled list of email addresses that covered four sheets of paper.

With the help of a local health-food store, we arranged for our somewhat press-ganged CSF members to make good their enthusiasm for the project by paying the fishermen a small fee in advance for their fish – a crucial part of the scheme being that the money is paid up front to help fund the fishermen's efforts.

The Cadgwith Community Supported Fishery had been born, and if it was not quite a bouncing baby then at least all the constituent parts seemed to be vaguely in the right place. We had a plentiful supply of crab and fish, an enthusiastic if slightly bewildered clientele and, thanks to Jonathan's fish shop, the ability to process the catch as and when required. Between painful birth and glorious maturity there would be many stumbling blocks, but at least we had begun.

* * *

Schemes such as Community Supported Fisheries are one of the potential paths that lead into the future. But to create this viable future, the fishing industry must first confront the demons of its past. Recent history is littered with tales of ravaged fishing grounds and unfettered fleets reaping a harvest on a terrible scale. Perhaps the most famous of these is the tragic tale of the Grand Banks, told to me during my brief visit to America by men who stared into the middle distance as they spoke, their minds gripped by the unfathomable loss of what had appeared to one and all to be an unlimited resource.

The Grand Banks off the southeastern coast of Newfoundland were a near-mythical place, where in 1497 the explorer John Cabot reported an abundance of fish so great that simply lowering a bucket into the sea would produce a catch. The elegant schooners out of Massachusetts wrote their name large in fishing folklore in the late 19th century, using baited hooks deployed from tiny dories crewed by brave men who paid a terrible price for their endeavours in this fog-bound El Dorado.

Such were the riches of the Banks that even many centuries of exploitation seemed to make little difference to the swarming shoals of cod that were the prize. Here was a robust, fecund species that appeared to have a limitless ability to recover. The estimate of the biomass of cod alone on the Banks was 1.5 million tons, an endlessly reproducing source of protein and wealth for the men who reaped the whirlwind far offshore.

Gradually the scale of the fishing effort increased: with the dawn of factory ships the Grand Banks were soon being harvested on a previously unimaginable scale. The fishing grounds became a floating city, a monument to man's ingenuity as a huge community of boats large and small mined the rich seams of fish below them day and night. Vast ships – not boats, but ships – weighing thousands of tons steamed in from Korea, from Europe and from Cuba. A cod could be caught, gutted, filleted and canned entirely at sea. The Grand Banks had become a hub for the international fishing effort, a model of industrial excellence. In 1968 alone, 810,000 tons of cod were caught, over half of the entire stock of the Grand Banks, in a 12-month period. An idea of the sheer scale of this fishing effort becomes apparent when one considers that the total annual catch of the global fishing fleet today is approximately 80 million tons – and yet this tiny patch of ocean produced one eightieth of that amount from a single species.

The Canadian Government could have halted this apocalyptic fishing effort by regulating the fleets, particularly after they declared a 200-mile coastal exclusion zone for foreign vessels in 1977. This encompassed much of the Grand Banks and allowed them a measure of control over what was – in glorious retrospect – a rare global asset. But the opportunity was missed, and the combination of a renewed fishing effort using Canadian boats, overly (some would say insanely) optimistic quotas and a reluctance to alienate voters in a suddenly prosperous Newfoundland, saw the fishing continue unabated.

'The fish stocks did not decline, they simply crashed into oblivion'

And then abruptly – the unthinkable. All man's ingenuity, all the computer guidance and acoustic technology, all the experience, all the horsepower and hydraulics were suddenly producing nothing. The fish stocks did not decline, they simply crashed into oblivion. A biological tipping point had been reached, a moment when the implacable attention of man overcame a survival strategy honed by millions of years of evolution. This vast fleet, so potent and powerful, had reaped an efficient and cold-blooded harvest of such scale and relentless ferocity that the cod – one of the great ocean survivors – had simply vanished in its wake. Not a patch of the fishing grounds had been left untrawled, not a shoal untouched and the great, swarming masses of the Grand Banks had at last been fished into a loose collection of stragglers that swam in empty seas. In 1992 – amid fury and denial from the Canadian fishing community – the government closed down the fishery. To this day it has yet to recover.

The Grand Banks had been a victim of a grotesque gold rush, the result of unregulated industrialisation spawned by competition between nations over a limited fishing area using larger and larger ships. It must never happen again – indeed it can never happen again as such seething abundance of any creature in the sea is now part of our history, consigned forever to the enthusiastic scrawlings of long-past pioneers and adventurers.

Perhaps the only example even vaguely similar is that of krill: even now the great global fishing fleets are turning south, leaving behind spent traditional grounds as they churn towards the promise of new bounty. We fish this krill at our peril, removing as we do one of the key building blocks for so many other fish species.

'Either we stop eating fish or we accept that the larger vessels must exist'

At the very heart of this is an age-old dilemma facing man as a hunter. If the quarry becomes elusive and sparse, then the solution has always been to increase the effort, to search longer and harder using the best technology available. And so as the cod shoals decreased in size, the ships hunting them grew in capability and dimensions. Fishing trips became longer and ventured further afield, tracking their prey with electronic assets that represented the cutting edge of technology – a pattern repeated in European waters and across the world. The result was a prey harried into oblivion, with nowhere to hide and no defence against the vessels that pursued it.

But there are also examples of fisheries that have prospered even today. The vast tracts of the southern Atlantic around the Falkland Islands and South Georgia are patrolled ruthlessly by the Royal Navy, and remain a model of sustainable exploitation. Then there are the lobster fisheries of Maine, where legislative power has been handed back to the fishing fleet, who duly defied all expectations by responsibly policing their own fishing efforts. Two examples – one of national gunboat diplomacy, the other of localised small-scale legislation – both showing that there is a way forward. What is obvious is that blind denial of the problem is simply not an option.

The point of this story is not to exclusively sing the praises of the small boats. There must remain a place for the larger boats in fishing today. Western governments set ambitious targets for fish consumption, urging consumers to gorge on a superfood, rich in oils that are said to boost intelligence. In 2011 the US Government raised the recommended consumption of seafood to 230 grams per person per week, more than twice the previous national average.

Essentially the powers-that-be in America – the same legislators who are responsible for conserving fish stocks – are actively encouraging their population to increase their demand for fish by 100 per cent. To supply such markets is beyond the capability of the small, traditional fishing boats, so we are faced with a stark choice. Either we stop eating fish or we accept that the larger vessels must exist. We desperately need to produce meaningful scientific data to show where and when target species can be fished and, in conjunction with the fishermen, to develop gear that reduces by-catch and discard. We cannot wring our hands and demand an end to large-scale fishing while at the same

time making sure our children eat plenty of fish, as is heartily endorsed by those who govern us.

America long ago acknowledged that all this fish cannot come from the oceans alone: of the 85 per cent of US seafood that is imported, approximately half comes from aquaculture. Once seen as the solution to the world's protein shortage and the saviour of global fish stocks, the reality of fish farming is mired in complexity and stealthy ecological impacts.

As wild stocks dwindle, there has been an explosion in the farming of fish for food. In 1950, the amount of fish produced globally by aquaculture was less than a million tons. By 2008, that figure had increased to 47.3 million tons. But with large-scale production come large-scale problems. A poorly run salmon farm of 200,000 fish produces the same amount of nitrates and phosphorus – essentially the by-products of sewage – as a town of 20,000 people. This injects a lethal quantity of nutrients into shallow coastal environments, creating food for unnatural blooms of algae that stifle and choke reefs and clear-water systems. Mangrove swamps – crucial nurseries for numerous fish species and a filter to sediment run-off from the land – have been cleared on a mass scale in Thailand to make way for shrimp farms.

Regrettably our craving for certain species tends to lean towards carnivorous fish – salmon and tuna being prime examples – and these are fed with fish meal. This means that for every kilogram of farmed fish, you need two kilograms of wild fish to feed them, leaving the oceans in what *Time* magazine pithily termed a 'situation of net loss'. China is responsible for 61 per cent of the world's fish produced by aquaculture and, as demand has increased, has been guilty of simply pushing more and more fish into the limited space of the old farms, leading to disease and pollution.

New programmes of integrated multitrophic aquaculture (IMTA) have been trialled with some success. These farms replicate a wild environment by having fish pens next to shellfish and seaweed facilities. The waste of one farm therefore feeds the other. These and other schemes show that there is a place for aquaculture – we have little choice, to be frank – but it is not the final solution to the vexing question of sustainability. It is here that legislation has been wielded to ensure longevity for both fish stocks and fishing boats, and it is here that the problem becomes apparent.

In the deluge of rules and regulations brought in to control the activities of larger vessels, the great strengths of the under-10-metre fleet have been ignored. Here are vessels with limited range that fish on a daily basis, that support local communities, that (on the whole) use static gear working traditional fishing grounds and that make up nearly 80 per cent of all our fishing vessels. The small-boat fleet's unique qualities – the freshness, sustainability and seasonality of their catch – epitomise everything we desire from our seafood.

And yet as the links between the people of Britain and the sea that surrounds them grow ever more tenuous, so we have lost the ability to nurture our small-boat fleet. If we continue to maintain this arc of indifference, we will lose these boats completely. It is tempting to wax lyrical about their culture and heritage, but the real tragedy is perhaps not what we would lose from the past, but what we would deny ourselves for the future.

You can almost imagine the scenario in the centuries to come, as brilliant scientists attempt to model the perfect fishing techniques to create minimum environmental impact for maximum social benefit. They would almost certainly visualise a large number of small boats, crewed singly or in pairs, working in co-operation with local communities and fishing designated areas using low-impact equipment. They would in fact create a theoretical model of our present small-boat fishing fleet and, no doubt shaking their heads at our short-sightedness, they would despair at its loss.

* * *

As my time in Cadgwith drew to a close, it was a future slightly closer to home that was occupying me in more ways than one. My girlfriend Tam and my dog Reuben had been living with me in the cove for several months, a vivid illustration for me of just how important family is to a fisherman. To throw open the door from a filthy day, to stamp the rain off the wellies and duly be met by an avalanche of enthusiastic dog and a delighted missus suddenly became the perfect end to any fishing trip. Tam would listen patiently to the stories of my heroics, would examine any scars sympathetically and would murmur appreciatively as I exaggerated the size and ferocity of the sea conditions.

There was also the moderately pressing matter of her being eight months' pregnant. I was vaguely aware of a whiff of rampant hormones in the air, mainly signified by a great deal of nest-building and hoovering. Reubs would peer out at me with wide eyes from under the kitchen table as the vacuum swept past yet again, aware that he was dealing with forces neither of us could possibly understand.

Fishing trips were made with the radio on maximum volume, waiting for that oh-so-significant call. Nige was delighted at my patent ignorance at what lay ahead, chuckling with pleasure every time I mentioned how tired I was finding a particular day's fishing.

'Tired? Tired? Ah, Mont, you've no idea, have you? Let's chat in about a month, shall we, then you'll have found out about being tired. Oh dear, oh dear.' And he would beam in delighted anticipation.

The call came not when I was out at sea, but in the form of being prodded awake one windy night at 4 a.m. by Tam saying that she felt 'surges'.

'Do you think we should go to hospital?' I said, with just the tiniest hint of alarm.

'No, not for now,' she replied. Vastly relieved, I muttered something that almost certainly involved the words 'chin up' and 'old girl', before instantly falling back to sleep.

When the next day dawned, it was unequivocal that things were afoot. One of the ladies in the village recommended a good walk along the cliff path and so we trudged up steep hills, Tam pausing occasionally to lean over with her hands on her knees as Reubs and I looked on as only two hairy, pointless males can in this type of situation. There is a special kind of ham-fisted helplessness experienced by a man watching his loved one writhe in pain at the imminent birth of their child, and I explored the complete tidal range of emotions over the next few hours.

Nige called regularly for updates, a calm, measured voice on the end of the phone that offered nothing but support and gentle encouragement. When I walked onto the beach the fishermen all enquired after Tam, with Philip even offering his services as a midwife using a net bin as an impromptu birthing pool. This was an offer I politely declined.

In a few more hours it was plainly time to call the hospital, who after a brief conversation said we should come in. This was it. This ... was ... it! I drove in with Tam groaning in the approved manner on the back seat. As the groans grew in intensity, so the needle of the speedometer climbed steadily into previously uncharted regions of the dial until I was performing the type of manoeuvre that gets Lewis Hamilton banned for several races. This was for two reasons – the first being a desperate urge to get her to hospital, the second, altogether more shameful one being that the Land Rover was a brand new one on loan and I had very real concerns about the hand-stitched seats.

On a cold, windswept evening we arrived in Treliske Hospital in Truro and passed into a wonderful world of competence and calm. Unbeknown to all three of us involved in this little drama, it would be another day before the baby would appear. Tam's contribution to this was to be steadfast, serene and strong as only a woman in labour can be – a monument to the power of nature. Mine was to put the cardboard wee pot on my head as a novelty hat in order to cheer her up during the darkest hour before the following dawn. This was swiftly removed as she assured me that it was 'not funny'. I retired huffily to the foot of the bed, reflecting on the fact that there is no pleasing some people.

Our daughter finally entered the world through Caesarean section, a moment forever imprinted on my memory. Tam was blissfully sedated, but I witnessed the entire operation and simply couldn't shake the impression of a fisherman trying to wrestle a particularly stubborn lobster out of a smallish pot. And then, after an effort that had lasted 36 hours and involved scores of people, our daughter – little Isla Grace – was placed in my arms. Covered in blood, puce and crumpled, she looked furious, a cross between an inebriated ginger Winston Churchill and a very sunburnt Alan Carr. She was also, without a doubt, the most beautiful thing I had ever seen.

Outside, only moments later, I called my mum, my dad and my sister. Then I called Nige.

* * *

To return to Cadgwith was to come home, entering into the warmth of a welcome that only a tight-knit community built on mutual support can muster. It was three weeks before Christmas and the cove shone with lights strung out over the sea and within the cliff walls. This was a long-standing tradition in the village and made it look particularly magical from seaward, the land around it plunged into darkness by the colours and intensity of the decorations. It glowed in the night, alive and vibrant, a beacon calling us home from the few short fishing trips we could manage in the ever-changing weather conditions.

Wetting the baby's head involved toasting her in the confines of the Cadgwith Cove Inn. This was a lengthy process and, having gathered a good head of steam, it seemed only natural that we should then toast the boats, the fish and anyone who happened to walk in. I glanced up from the bar to see Nige, Dom, Tonks, Danny, Louis and Worm all chatting animatedly in the throng, and felt a huge surge of gratitude that they had turned out to welcome Isla into the cove. This was something that made me very happy indeed, although by this stage of the evening most things were

'To return to Cadgwith
was to come home'

making me happy in a burpy, beaming kind of way.

Walks through the village now took on considerable logistical significance. Before having a baby, I had absolutely no idea that leaving the house with one required a similar amount of kit to a Victorian siege-style expedition on Annapurna, but that seemed to be unequivocally the case. Shy debutante parents that we were, we would push our brand new pram down to where the boats were pulled up on the beach and find doors being flung open along the road and local people coming out to hug Tam and admire little Isla. This community had almost imperceptibly become a hugely important part of my life. I was immensely proud that our daughter – wherever she went and whatever she did for the rest of her life – would always be a Cadgwith girl.

* * *

The Community Supported Fishery was quietly developing as the Christmas break approached. Nige, Jonathan and I had a plan that involved a final fishing trip, catching a range of species in conjunction with Danny, Louis, Dom and Tonks, and then using this catch as the basis for our hand-out the next day. It was imperative that the fish we distributed were fresh, that they were drawn from species that were not standard fare from the large supermarkets and – as Cadgwith was predominantly a shellfish fleet – that they were accompanied by a large crab for every consumer.

All was proceeding in surprisingly good order. You could sense the ground swell of interest in the cove, matched by the slow ignition of genuine curiosity among the people of Helston at the activities of the Cadgwith boats – which in so many respects was, of course, 'their' fleet. The only factor disrupting this otherwise rosy scene was the weather.

Poring over the weather reports became an obsession with me: they seemed to consist entirely of spiralling storm systems, mountains of wind driven on by tight contours of low pressure. Born in the vast open spaces of the Atlantic they might well be, but they all seemed to be uncannily intent on travelling straight over the top of Cadgwith.

Day after grey day passed, the boats locked onto the beach by wind and wave. Even when the main storm had passed a persistent ground swell remained, racing ahead of the next weather system many thousands of miles away, to be channelled by the high walls of the cove, thumping and growling along the cliffs in flecked ranks. It was impressive, all this energy created beyond the horizon, but with the fish hand-out for the Community Supported Fishery only days away its grandeur was somewhat lost on me.

After yet another frustrating day, my phone bleeped into life one evening with a short message from Nige – 'On for tomorrow – see you at 7.15 on the beach.' There was a window, a brief moment of calm, and the fleet would be thundering out of the cove the next morning as a mini armada, intent on a final foray before the end of the fishing season.

The plan was simplicity itself. Nige would not be fishing on *Razorbill*, but instead would use her as a chase boat (albeit one that had to ask the boats he was chasing to slow down so he could catch up). He would ferry me from Dom and Louis' boat – who had teamed up for this last trip – onto *Kingfisher 2* to join Tonks, then we would all return to the beach to pick through Danny's catch. So I would leave the cove after a single day's fishing

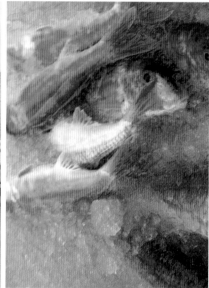

with a clicking tub of crabs and a very impressive range of fish species for the big hand-out the next day.

The next morning worked seamlessly for at least the first three minutes, until *Razorbill* broke down. This didn't happen very often – in fact it had never happened in my entire time in the cove – however when it did Nige had to deal not only with fixing the problem, but with the combined input of Louis and Dom leaning over the rail of their boat alongside, offering advice.

By the time we arrived on the scene, Nige was bobbing about at the mouth of the cove rummaging in the engine compartment. The only target available for abuse was his oilskin-clad backside. This seemed absolutely fine for Louis and Dom, who fired alternating verbal volleys as they surveyed the scene.

'Roight, Nige, you need an 11mm spanner for this one, I'd say,' said Louis, after inspecting the problem, knowing perfectly well that Nige didn't have one – or any spanners, for that matter. 'I can lend you one if you ask nicely.'

'Have you considered that the reason you've broken down is that you're always nicking diesel from any old canister on the beach, Nige?' asked Dom in an entirely reasonable voice. 'And that one of them might have had rainwater in?'

I suspect Nige would have stormed off if possible, but short of making a swim for it his choices were limited. He opted instead for a dignified silence. He didn't even say anything when – to my considerable surprise – I found myself joining in. I comforted myself with the thought that if the roles had been reversed Nige would definitely have given me plenty of stick, and he was a sitting duck, after all.

After much debate, and with the day slipping away, it was decided that the best option was to give *Razorbill* a tow.

'Although the fact that you have to tow your chase boat does mean it's somewhat limited in performing its role, wouldn't you say, Nige?' said Dom.

'Technically I'm still chasing you, though,' said Nige, with what I thought was a fair amount of elan under the circumstances. Moments later, as he bounced along in our wake, he caught a pollack by trailing a lure over the side of *Razorbill*'s transom. This he waved in triumph at Louis and Dom in a 'not-quite-so-chirpy-now-are-you-chaps' manner.

The fishing proved to be surprisingly good. Nets that had been set only a few hours before yielded cod, gurnard, the occasional red mullet, bib, a few thumping pollack and even a bass.

'I think I'll probably hang on to this one, Mont,' said Louis, as he placed the bass in a fish box with a conspiratorial grin. 'The Community Supported Fishery can muddle by without it, I'd say.'

Strangely enough, this was precisely the point of the project. Everyone knows that the bass is a beautiful, valuable fish. What we were trying to do was give value to the species that are normally worthless, in the process educating people about the taste and texture of fish they wouldn't generally eat.

I was entirely happy to rummage through the catch, setting aside beautiful, fresh, seasonal fish. This too was an important part of the CSF, catching species that were naturally found off our coastline at this time of year. They had sculled into nets set only a few hundred metres offshore, and required no more transport costs than a few litres of petrol in Nige's van to get them to Helston. Set these same nets in the same place in a few months' time and you would catch a whole new range of fish species, providing the seasonal variety that our diet used to experience, before the advent of long-distance trawlers and air freight.

The transfer to Tonks' boat proved moderately exciting in sea conditions that even he reluctantly described as 'lively'. There was one truly thrilling moment when I had one foot on Louis' boat and one on Tonks' as both moved energetically in opposite directions, causing me to emit a muffled falsetto squeal of anticipation. Fortunately the swell threw them back together, leaving me with a sense of mild relief that I had already fathered a child. Tonks had hauled a few strings of pots and had several tubs full of cock crabs.

'Above all the fishermen of Cadgwith – these men who made their perilous living off the Lizard – were survivors'

These I inspected, setting aside the best ones for the hand-out. Tonks peered over my shoulder, occasionally pointing out a particularly fine specimen. He had an expert's eye for a crab in good condition and didn't subscribe to my 'big is definitely best' theory. He would pick out a crab of medium size, press it with thumbs the shape of plump sausages and peer into the middle distance with brow furrowed before tossing it to one side and picking up the next.

Soon the bin was full of beautiful, healthy crabs. Their brown carapaces shone like burnished copper, slick with the cold Atlantic water from which they had been plucked only minutes before. All that remained was to meet Danny on the beach

to select a few fish from his catch, and we were ready to go.

As we turned for home, I had a moment of sudden realisation. This was my final trip, the last time I would stand on the deck of a Cadgwith boat and watch the Todden slip by as we rode the swells towards the beach. As the bow hit the shingle, I glanced across at Tonks in the wheelhouse, intent on the job in hand, filthy cap perched on the back of his head. He looked invincible, defiant in the face of the vast odds facing any modern small-boat fisherman.

As I jumped from the bow one last time to walk up the beach and start the winch, I reflected that there was something comforting in that defiance. It might be my last trip, but there is still a hint of the vagabond in a Cadgwith fisherman that brought home to me their eminent capacity for survival. For centuries they had adapted and evolved to the system of governance, whether it be in the imaginative use of cubby holes in a cottage of yesteryear, or the use of every ounce of fishing skill and flexibility in varying their target species today. As I hooked up the winch to *Kingfisher 2* I knew that above all other things the fishermen of Cadgwith – these men who made their perilous living off the Lizard – were survivors.

After I met Danny on the beach and sorted through his catch, the moment came for the fishermen to be paid for the glistening box of fish at my feet. The beauty of the CSF is that, without the transport and processing costs of their normal outlets, they would get considerably more than the usual prices – and this for species that would normally be very difficult to sell. It seemed to me, as we loaded the fish and crabs into the cold store to be picked up the next day, that the best ideas are invariably the simplest.

The next afternoon Nige, Jonathan and I piled the fish into his van and drove the 10 miles or so into Helston. This was the final act in the drama for me, a chance to create the smallest of bridges between a local Cornish community and their fishermen. There was a slight moment of chagrin after we had set the catch on the table, a pregnant pause during which no one turned up and I feared the whole exercise might be for naught. And then, striding towards us out of the gathering gloom of a December evening, came our first customer. She was a formidable-looking lady of a certain age accompanied by her two grandchildren, both of whom skipped and danced with excitement as they approached the table. Nige smiled as they drew near and reached into the tub of ice at his feet to pull out a large cod.

'How about this for your weekly fish?' he said to her, waving it in her direction. The children's eyes widened at the wonder of it all, staring at this great speckled monster with eyes like doubloons and a bristly chin. They were just as excited about the fish he was holding. Jonathan was not far behind, reaching into the tub of crabs to pull out a scarred old male, legs weaving and claws clicking.

This was – certainly as far as the children were concerned – the greatest thing that had ever happened in the history of everything anywhere. These were probably the very first fishermen they had ever met and they must have looked like heroes from another age, with their gold earrings and bright yellow oilskins. Soon Nige and Jonathan were vying for air-time, chatting animatedly to the family about the ways of crabs and of fish, about deep water and cold dawns.

As the evening progressed, more and more people turned up for their hand-out

of fresh fish, to leave moments later clutching plastic bags containing wondrous new species and muttering suggested recipes. It seemed to me, watching from the sidelines, that every handover was a little triumph.

Before me was the very essence of the Community Supported Fishery. There was every chance that this particular scheme would come to nothing – certainly our hand-out was on such a small scale it was negligible. But then again there was the consoling factor that the CSF schemes in America had grown from a few enthusiastic churchgoers into a national phenomenon, so who knows what the future might hold here in Cornwall? It was an exciting thought, but the real pleasure lay in watching Nige and Jonathan – two fishermen telling tall tales to local people, describing a way of life that as smartly dressed office workers they could only imagine. It was as if we had produced – just for a moment – a sepia image of a time when fishermen were revered and respected.

* * *

How do we save these men and this ancient fleet, the last hunter-gatherers remaining in our island? Over my time working with the boats large and small I had realised that the array of administrative and legislative measures was suffocating what little life remained in the industry. There seem to be only two things universally acknowledged by the scientists, the government and the fishermen themselves. The first is that present legislation is ineffective and needs radical alteration. The second is that fish stocks need protecting.

For me it seems entirely logical that we introduce areas where fishing activity should be limited or indeed stopped altogether. This has been shown throughout history to be effective – with catches rising dramatically in the North Sea after both wars in the last century as the conflicts curtailed fishing activity. This view is shared by the government, who in 2009 introduced a bill to explore the viability of Marine Conservation Zones (MCZs).

Predictably this ambitious scheme has become somewhat mired in controversy and in-fighting, with the deadline for the findings of the numerous study groups set up around the British coast recently extended until 2013. Scientific and conservation groups are at odds with local fleets, with accusations of sly malpractice and outright deception hurled back and forth between the organisations involved.

'We must rediscover our connection with our fishing fleet'

Surely we cannot squander this last-ditch opportunity to save both our fish stocks and our fishing fleet? In designating MCZs we must be aware that we potentially deprive small-boat fishermen of their livelihood and acknowledge that compensation will be necessary for the time needed for the zones to take effect. This may be over the course of many years, but in the process we just may extend the life of the fleet to the next generation and beyond, a priceless gift to our national heritage and our proud seafaring traditions. It is imperative that the scientific data is sound, but it is equally imperative that the fishermen adhere to such findings.

Amid the clarion calls for the fishermen

to change their habits and their lifestyle, we ignore the fact that it is of equal significance that we do the same. We must rediscover our connection with our fishing fleet. In my opinion it is entirely nonsensical for British families to eat so much fish from overseas and to have become drones at the behest of marketing machines that ensure we eat only certain species in certain packaging.

There is a vast array of flavours and textures in the seas that surround our island, and the fact that we throw so much of it away is all down to cultural programming. I yearn for the day when we awaken that distant hunter-gatherer in us all and eat seasonal fish caught close to shore by sustainable means. It would be an adventure, a sensory voyage into our past and one that we are all entirely equipped to undertake. In doing so we would ease the pressure on a few desperately over-exploited species, reduce discard and waste, and maybe – just maybe – save a way of life that does so much to define us.

* * *

Last day, and the final trudge down the hill towards the beach. I stopped briefly by the Todden, looking down on the boats pulled up high on the beach below. It was a beautiful, crisp, still December morning, one of those days that heightens the senses and fogs the breath. There was hardly a whisper of wind, the last storm having charged towards the east carrying its violence and fury to new inlets and new harbours. The water clopped and gurgled into the gullies and hollows of the cove walls, sounding almost metallic in the clear air. Glancing at the roof of the Cadgwith Cove Inn, I could see the customary row of gulls peering out to sea like some sombre parliament, feathers puffed up and eyes

half shut as they basked in the weak winter sunshine.

Nige was in his shed and muttered a barely decipherable hello as I tapped on the door. He was sitting surrounded by a pile of half-finished withy pots and glanced up with a smile as I shut the door behind me. The pots looked like the skeletal remains of some strange sea creature scattered around the floor of the shed, with Nige in their midst like a benign Neptune. He rose to his feet, grimacing slightly as he did so. There was a moment of silence, an awkward beat that hung briefly in the air. Nige dealt with this in his inimitable style.

'Well, Mont,' he said, 'this'll be you buggering off, then.'

'I am indeed buggering off, Nige,' I said. 'I think I've taught you all I can.'

He snorted in delight.

'Yep, that'd be right. Nothing else you can teach me. I'm probably ready to go fishing on my own now.'

There was another brief pause. I glanced at the scene around me.

'You'll give me a call if you need a hand with the withy pots, won't you, Nige?' I said.

Another snort of laughter.

'That too,' he said. 'No idea how I'll get by without you, quite frankly. Come on, I'll walk with you down to the beach.'

We walked in companionable silence out to where the boats sat quietly on the shingle, engines stilled and decks ordered. The end of the crabbing season had arrived a few days earlier and there was an air of tranquillity about the place, a million miles from the normal frenetic activity that surrounded the fleet.

'Well, Nige, this is me,' I said, pointing back up the hill to where the Land Rover waited, loaded to the gunwales and parked symbolically pointing east – away from the Lizard, away from Cadgwith and away from my life as a fisherman.

'You got everything? Been to the toilet? Got some flares in case I need to come and get you?' said Nige with a smile, before turning to look at the boats.

'You've done well, you know,' he said, gazing over the fleet as he spoke. 'I just can't imagine this cove without these boats and these men. It's important that you tell our story, because once they're gone from here, they'll never come back. I know it's just a few little crabbers, but they're important to us.'

'Me too, Nige,' I said, and meant it.

'Well, off you go, then. Good luck to you and drop me a line if you ever fancy a trip out.' He smiled and extended his hand for a final shake.

'Yeah, I'll do that, Nige,' I replied, and meant that too.

This great man had guided me through months of fishing out of this ancient cove. With endless patience he had taught me about the ways of the sea, and in doing so had given me so much more than I could ever have garnered from any book or lecture. I was leaving with a profound respect for him and his ilk.

I strode towards the steep hill out of the cove for the final time. Past the boats, past Danny's net loft, past the winch house and back to my life. I glanced back just the once as I rounded the corner and saw that Nige had remained by the side of *Razorbill*. He raised one hand in farewell, then turned back to the boat to lift a coil of line and begin to loop it into a barrel at his feet. Apprentices come and go, but there is always the next neap tide, the next period of calm and the next string of pots to haul from the cold, violent waters off Black Head.

Fish Buying Guide

Buying fish is a minefield, but if we want to carry on enjoying it then we need to make smart choices at the supermarket and fishmonger. This chart shows the Marine Conservation Society's advice on what to eat and not eat using a 'traffic light' system, and indicates the months when species are considered in season and no longer spawning. Fresh fish, caught from the sea or wild stocks, should be eaten outside of the spawning season and above the size at which they mature – check details at www.fishonline.org; some species of fish are farmed and therefore available all year. If you're buying frozen fish, you can still check for the catch area and if it's been certified by a responsible organisation. Although the chart advises on the best choices, food packaging is not required by law to state how fish has been caught (see page 251), so to be sure you're buying the most sustainable and environmentally friendly fish ask your retailer how and where it was caught. If they don't know, don't buy it.

- • best sustainable choice
- • stocks are at risk or recovering
- • to be avoided due to overfishing and/or poor management and/or damaging fishing methods
- * indicates species indigenous to UK waters

Abbreviations:

- MSC Marine Stewardship Council
- MCS Marine Conservation Society
- IUCN International Union for Conservation of Nature
- FAD Fish Aggregating Device

Species	Jan	Feb	Mar	Apr	May	June	July	Aug	Sept	Oct	Nov	Dec
Anchovy — Best choice: fish from the Bay of Biscay where stocks are at sustainable levels.	•	•	•	•	•				•	•	•	•
Brill* — Avoid due to overfishing and unsustainability.	•	•	•						•	•	•	•
Brown crab* — Buy pot-caught crab.				•	•	•	•	•	•	•	•	
Brown/sea trout* — Buy wild sea trout only from an Environment Agency-licensed net fishery – retailers stock only licensed fish but you will need to ask in restaurants. Brown trout is farmed; buy organically farmed.				•	•	•	•	•	•	•		
Brown shrimp — Best choice: shrimp caught by trawls fitted with veil nets and separators.	•	•	•							•	•	•
Catfish/pangasius — A farmed fish; look for GlobalGAP certification which ensures environmental standards are met during farming.	•	•	•	•	•	•	•	•	•	•	•	•

Species	Jan	Feb	Mar	Apr	May	June	July	Aug	Sept	Oct	Nov	Dec
Clams — Several species available (some indigenous to the UK). Best choice: sustainably farmed or hand harvested from wild stocks.	•	•	•	•	•	•	•	•	•	•	•	•
Cockles* — Buy hand gathered from legal fisheries – some people mass-collect them from beaches and illegally sell them on.									•	•	•	•
Cod* (Atlantic) — Buy line caught with an MSC tick logo. Check fishonline.org for the most sustainable stocks.	•			•	•	•	•	•	•	•	•	•
Coley* — Buy line caught with an MSC tick logo. Check fishonline.org for the most sustainable stocks.						•	•	•	•	•	•	•
Dab* — A by-catch fish and a great alternative to more vulnerable flatfish species such as plaice.	•	•	•				•	•	•	•	•	•
Dover sole* — Health of stocks vary: check the latest advice from fishonline.org. Best choice: fish from the English Channel with an MSC tick logo.	•			•	•	•			•	•	•	•
Eel — Avoid all eels; even farming requires the capture and use of wild juveniles, known as glass eels.	•	•	•	•	•	•	•	•	•	•	•	•
Flounder* — A by-catch fish and a more sustainable alternative to vulnerable flatfish species such as plaice.			•			•	•	•	•	•	•	•
Gurnard* (grey and red) — A by-catch fish with white, meaty flesh. Tub or yellow varieties (•).	•	•	•									
Haddock* — Buy line caught with an MSC tick logo. Check latest stock levels at fishonline.org.	•	•		•	•	•	•	•	•	•	•	•

Hake* (European)
The northern European stock (generally for the UK market) is well managed and sustainable. Avoid hake from southern European stock which is overfished.

Halibut (Atlantic)
Buy onshore farmed halibut. Wild-caught Atlantic and Greenland halibut should be completely avoided (●).

Herring*
There are various sustainable fisheries in Europe and the UK. Look for the MSC tick logo.

John Dory*
A by-catch fish. Stocks aren't managed or regulated so juvenile fish can make it to your plate (avoid any under 25cm).

Langoustine* (scampi)
Buy pot caught rather than trawled.

Lemon sole*
Best choice: Lemon sole landed in Cornwall or caught using seine nets.

Ling*
Buy line caught and local fish rather than ling trawled by deep-water fisheries. Check fishonline.org for the most sustainable stocks.

Lobster* (European)
Lobster fisheries are licensed but choose those that are pot caught rather than netted. Shell length should be no less than 9cm.

Mackerel*
Buy fish caught using traditional methods (handline, ring net or drift net) with an MSC tick logo.

Species	Jan	Feb	Mar	Apr	May	June	July	Aug	Sept	Oct	Nov	Dec
Hake	●				●	●	●	●	●	●	●	●
Halibut	●	●	●	●	●	●						
Herring	●	●	●	●	●	●	●	●	●	●	●	●
John Dory	●	●	●	●	●				●	●	●	●
Langoustine	●	●		●	●	●						●
Lemon sole	●	●	●					●	●	●	●	
Ling	●	●						●	●	●	●	
Lobster	●	●	●	●	●				●	●	●	
Mackerel	●	●					●	●	●	●		

Monkfish*
Buy fish caught by tangle nets. Check fishonline.org for the most sustainable stocks.

Mussels*
Widely farmed; buy rope-grown mussels. If buying wild mussels, ensure they have been hand gathered and not dredged.

Oysters*
Buy farmed native or Pacific oysters.

Plaice*
A long-lived species and subject to high fishing pressure. Avoid and choose dab or flounder instead.

Pollack*
Great alternative to cod and haddock. Choose line caught and tagged (those caught by handline in Cornwall are tagged).

Pouting/bib*
A by-catch fish and a good cod alternative.

Prawns (cold water/northern)
Cold-water prawns or shrimps are more sustainable than tropical, trawled prawns. Best choice: MSC certified from Canada – look for the tick logo.

Prawns (warm water/king and tiger)
Wild caught and non-certified farmed king and tiger prawns should be avoided. Best choice: organically farmed (●).

Rainbow trout
Most rainbow trout available in the UK is farmed. Best choice: organically farmed.

Red mullet*
Best choice: fish caught by gill or seine net.

Species	Jan	Feb	Mar	Apr	May	June	July	Aug	Sept	Oct	Nov	Dec
Monkfish	●	●						●	●	●	●	●
Mussels	●	●	●	●	●	●	●	●	●	●	●	●
Oysters	●	●	●	●						●	●	●
Plaice					●	●	●	●	●	●	●	●
Pollack					●	●	●	●	●	●	●	●
Pouting/bib	●	●						●	●	●	●	
Prawns (cold water)		●	●	●	●	●	●	●			●	●
Prawns (warm water)	●	●	●	●	●	●	●	●	●	●	●	●
Rainbow trout												
Red mullet	●	●	●	●					●	●	●	●

	Jan	Feb	Mar	Apr	May	June	July	Aug	Sept	Oct	Nov	Dec

Salmon*

Atlantic farmed salmon is widely available; look for the Freedom Food logo. Best choice: organically farmed (•). Stocks of wild-caught Atlantic salmon are severely depleted and should be avoided (•). Wild-caught Pacific salmon are sustainable.

Jan	Feb	Mar	Apr	May	June	July	Aug	Sept	Oct	Nov	Dec
•	•	•	•	•	•	•	•	•	•	•	•

Sardines/pilchards*

Best choice: Cornish sardines caught using traditional drift or ring nets.

Jan	Feb	Mar	Apr	May	June	July	Aug	Sept	Oct	Nov	Dec
•	•					•	•	•	•	•	

Scallops

Buy dive-caught (king) or otter-trawled scallops (queen). If not labelled, queen scallops are smaller and generally sold as meat only; king scallops have the roe attached.

Jan	Feb	Mar	Apr	May	June	July	Aug	Sept	Oct	Nov	Dec
•	•	•					•	•	•	•	

Sea bass*

Best choice: line caught (especially handline from Cornwall and Devon); also look for gill-netted fish from northeast England with an MSC tick logo. Avoid sea bass caught by pelagic trawl (•) – by-catch caught by this method can include dolphins.

Jan	Feb	Mar	Apr	May	June	July	Aug	Sept	Oct	Nov	Dec
•	•					•	•	•	•	•	•

Sea bream/black bream/porgy*

Buy line or gill-netted fish caught and landed from Cornwall, northwestern and north Wales or Sussex.

Jan	Feb	Mar	Apr	May	June	July	Aug	Sept	Oct	Nov	Dec
•	•	•				•	•	•	•	•	•

Skate/ray*

Skate and ray belong to the same family; both are slow to grow and breed and therefore vulnerable to fishing. Avoid all but the smaller breeds of spotted, cuckoo or starry ray.

Jan	Feb	Mar	Apr	May	June	July	Aug	Sept	Oct	Nov	Dec
•	•	•	•	•	•	•	•	•	•	•	•

Dogfish/rock salmon/huss

The northeast Atlantic stock is critically endangered. Avoid eating this fish.

Jan	Feb	Mar	Apr	May	June	July	Aug	Sept	Oct	Nov	Dec
•	•	•	•	•	•	•	•	•	•	•	•

Spider crab*

Buy pot-caught crabs rather than those caught by tangle netting.

Jan	Feb	Mar	Apr	May	June	July	Aug	Sept	Oct	Nov	Dec
•	•	•					•	•	•	•	•

Squid* (common)

Buy squid caught using jigging (jigs are a type of lure) from small-scale fisheries.

Jan	Feb	Mar	Apr	May	June	July	Aug	Sept	Oct	Nov	Dec
					•	•	•	•	•	•	•

Sturgeon and caviar

Wild sturgeon are close to extinction – hardly surprising when some breeds live up to 100 years and it takes 10 years for a fish to reach maturity.

Jan	Feb	Mar	Apr	May	June	July	Aug	Sept	Oct	Nov	Dec
•	•	•	•	•	•	•	•	•	•	•	•

Swordfish

Swordfish has a low resilience to fishing and is subject to high fishing pressure. Buy only swordfish from the northeast Pacific with an MSC tick logo (•).

Jan	Feb	Mar	Apr	May	June	July	Aug	Sept	Oct	Nov	Dec
•	•	•						•	•	•	•

Tilapia

Best choice: organically farmed.

Jan	Feb	Mar	Apr	May	June	July	Aug	Sept	Oct	Nov	Dec
•	•	•	•	•	•	•	•	•	•	•	•

Tuna (albacore)

Best choice: albacore caught by troll, jig or pole and line with an MSC tick logo from the north or south Pacific.

Jan	Feb	Mar	Apr	May	June	July	Aug	Sept	Oct	Nov	Dec
						•	•	•	•	•	

Tuna (bigeye)

Bigeye is larger and slower growing than other breeds of tuna and more vulnerable to fishing. Pacific bigeye is IUCN listed as endangered. Best choice: trolled fish from the Indian Ocean.

Jan	Feb	Mar	Apr	May	June	July	Aug	Sept	Oct	Nov	Dec
					•	•	•	•	•	•	•

Tuna (bluefin)

Slow growing and long lived so prone to overfishing. Stocks are in a critical state. Avoid this fish.

Jan	Feb	Mar	Apr	May	June	July	Aug	Sept	Oct	Nov	Dec
•	•	•	•	•	•	•	•	•	•	•	•

Tuna (skipjack)

Skipjack grow much faster than other breeds of tuna making it a more sustainable choice. Best choice – pole and line caught. Check fishonline.org for more details.

Jan	Feb	Mar	Apr	May	June	July	Aug	Sept	Oct	Nov	Dec
•	•	•	•	•	•	•	•	•	•	•	•

	Jan	Feb	Mar	Apr	May	June	July	Aug	Sept	Oct	Nov	Dec
Tuna (yellowfin)	•	•	•	•	•	•	•	•	•	•	•	•
Turbot*	•	•	•						•	•	•	•
Whiting*	•	•			•	•	•	•	•	•	•	

Tuna (yellowfin)

Best choice: those caught by troll, pole and line or by non-FAD associated purse seine methods from the Indian Ocean. Yellowfin is often a substitute for bluefin as its stocks are in better shape. Check fishonline.org for more details.

Turbot*

Turbot fishing isn't managed so little is known about its stocks but avoid beam-trawled fish. Best choice: farmed (•).

Whiting*

The status of many stocks is unknown or at an historical low. Whiting are mainly a by-catch species and fisheries suffer from high discard rates, which can be up to 80 per cent.

Information supplied courtesy of the Marine Conservation Society. Up-to-date details on stock levels and further information can be found online at www.fishonline.org
© Marine Conservation Society 2012

Fish labels – What to Look For

When you're buying fillets or whole fish (whether fresh, frozen, packaged or loose) at the supermarket or from a fishmonger the following should be clearly labelled in line with UK legislation:

• The commercial name of the fish

• Whether the fish was caught at sea, in inland waters or farmed

• Where the fish was caught; this will either be the country of production or a specific ocean area

The method of capture is not yet required on labelling but increasingly you will find that the more positive and sustainable methods are listed – if in doubt, ask. If your retailer doesn't know, walk away or buy a different, more sustainable species of fish you can be confident about. Processed fish, which includes fish fingers and canned fish, is currently exempt from these rules, although some packaging will include the information.

Logos and Certification

Legislation may still have some way to go but as a consumer you can also look for logos from the following bodies:

Freedom Food

This is a farm assurance and food labelling scheme run by the RSPCA. The scheme works to improve the welfare of farm animals reared for food – which includes farmed species of inland fish such as salmon and trout. Almost all of the major supermarkets stock products that are in the scheme – look for the round blue and white logo.

Dolphin Safe and Dolphin Friendly

The Earth Island Institute (EII), among many other environmental projects, campaigns for fishing methods that do not involve the deliberate hunting and capture of dolphins. EII's standards are stringent and companies have to sign up to the project and adhere to strict guidelines in order to call themselves 'dolphin safe'. Surprisingly, a universal logo is only now taking shape so you shouldn't necessarily be suspicious of differing logos. See earthisland.org/dolphinSafeTuna/consumer/ for more information and to check which companies are certified by EII.

Marine Stewardship Council (MSC)

The MSC is an independent, non-profit organisation that runs a sustainable certification scheme. Any wild-capture fishery (the scheme excludes farmed fish) from anywhere in the world can request assessment, but only those meeting the MSC's criteria can use their logo. Fundamentally the fisheries are required to minimise their environmental impact and manage stocks effectively to ensure they are indefinitely sustainable. Fisheries are re-assessed every five years. Look for the blue and white fish/tick logo.

Organic Certification

There are a number of approved bodies that can provide organic certification. Logos you'll more commonly come across on (farmed) fish packaging belong to the Soil Association and the Organic Food Federation. Both of these organisations regularly assess producers to ensure they meet EU criteria for organic accreditation.

INDEX

INDEX

PICTURE CREDITS

The AA wishes to thank the following photographers and organisations for their assistance in the preparation of this book. Abbreviations for the picture credits are as follows – (t) top; (b) bottom; (l) left; (r) right; (c) centre; (AA) AA World Travel Library

Front and Back Cover: AA/J Tims. Endpapers AA/J Tims; 1 Marea Downey; 2-3 Marea Downey; 5 Alex Smith; 6-7 Scott Jessop; 9 Paul David Drabble/Alamy; 11 AA/J Tims; 12-13 Marea Downey; 15 Marea Downey; 17tl AA/J Tims; 17tr Monty Halls; 17cl AA/J Tims; 17c Indus Films; 17r Marea Downey; 17bl Gary Eastwood Photography/Alamy; 17br Indus Films; 18-19 AA/John Wood; 20 Marea Downey; 23 Marea Downey; 25tl natureslight/Alamy; 25tr Gary K Smith/FLPA; 25cl AA/J Tims; 25c Marea Downey; 25cr Lee Pengelly/Silverscene Photography; 25bl Monty Halls; 25br Marea Downey; 26 Monty Halls; 28tl AA/J Tims; 28tr Luke Pavey/Indus Films; 28cl Luke Pavey/Indus Films; 28c AA/J Tims; 28cr Marea Downey; 28bl Jamie Balment/Indus Films; 28br Marea Downey; 33 AA/J Tims; 34 Marea Downey; 37tl David Chapman/ardea.com; 37tr Alan Curtis; 37cl AA/J Tims; 37c Luke Pavey/Indus Films; 37cr AA/J Tims; 37bl Bob Gibbons/ardea.com; 37br Marea Downey; 38-39 Marea Downey; 41 Marea Downey; 44-45 Monty Halls; 46 AA/J Tims; 51tl Marea Downey; 51tr Marea Downey; 51cl Marea Downey; 51c Jamie Balment/Indus Films; 51cr AA/John Wood; 51bl Marea Downey; 51br AA/J Tims; 52 Luke Pavey/Indus Films; 54tl Marea Downey; 54tr AA/John Wood; 54cl AA/John Wood; 54c Jamie Balment/Indus Films; 54cr Jamie Balment/Indus Films; 54bl Marea Downey; 54br Marea Downey; 57 Monty Halls; 59tl Monty Halls; 59tr Indus Films; 59cl AA/J Tims; 59c AA/J Tims; 59cr Marea Downey;

ACKNOWLEDGEMENTS

To attempt a project such as this alone would simply be impossible. At every stage of this process I was advised, assisted, encouraged and inspired by those around me.

Many thanks to Indus Productions and to Nick Shearman for their support and creating this concept in the first place. To Leona Cowley and Emma Haskins – you have the hardest job of any of us on a shoot like this, trying to steady the financial and administrative ship when so many demands are made on you from all sides. Steve Robinson was a firm hand on the tiller and a source of support throughout – I hope one day you get to go surfing and live the dream. Many thanks as well to the film crew, all of whom – rather annoyingly – had much better sea legs than I did. James Smith – the Ginger Badger – drove the production along very nicely on the front line. Jamie Balment is a truly great talent, and will be a name we all hear for many years to come. Thanks to Richard Farish for not only being an outstanding cameraman, but also a top bloke and very, very funny. Sometimes on purpose. And Luke Pavey applied himself relentlessly to the task. He may be permanently glued to the camera, and come from the Forest of Dean, but at heart he is a Cornish crab fisherman. If there was one person the skippers would have had to stay behind, it was probably him.

Whilst researching this book I leaned very heavily on two publications. The first was *Atlantic* by Simon Winchester, the tale of a great ocean written by a great author. The second book was *An Unnatural History of the Sea* by Callum Roberts – as close to a definitive history of man's impact on the sea as it is possible to find. These are two wonderful books, and I commend them to you.

Thanks to the brilliant Helen Brocklehurst from AA publishing – it's been a roller coaster ride but then again they're quite fun aren't they? Thanks also to Julian Alexander for setting it all up in the first place.

To the crew of the *Billy Rowney* – Steve, Danny, Charlie and Jamie – you are genuine men of the sea, and showed extraordinary tolerance to me when I was onboard. Thanks to all the fishermen we worked with throughout the eight months – on *Harvester*, *Valhalla*, and the *Lady Hamilton*. I was never treated with anything other than the warmest hospitality throughout.

To Marea Downey for providing images that are the very essence of Cadgwith and the Lizard. She is a rare talent, and cares passionately about Cadgwith and the future of the fleet, a passion that is reflected in her photographs.

Cadgwith became our home, and I must thank the people who live there for their great kindness and patience during what was a lengthy production. They live in a very special community. From the first day they made us feel truly welcome – they are all a great credit to a great village. We're so proud that Isla will always be a good Cadgwith lass.

Thanks to the maternity wing of Treliske Hospital – angels indeed. To the miraculous Suze – thanks for holding the fort so capably. My heartfelt thanks as ever to my Tam – you are my absolute rock.

Thanks to the skippers in the cove, for their endless decency, advice and good humour. It was a real pleasure and privilege to learn about your way of life.

And finally thanks to Nige and Ann. Of the many great things about this eight months, perhaps the very best was getting to know them.